HOUSE

PHILIPPA LEWIS

HOUSE
British Domestic Architecture

PRESTEL

MUNICH · LONDON · NEW YORK

Opposite page: Victorian eclecticism: red-brick terrace with Gothic Revival detail over the paired front doors; roof with iron cresting in the style of the French Second Empire and Dutch-inspired gables. Development, c. 1890. Highbury, North London.

Introduction

'**An Englishman's house is his castle, and ... the ownership of land includes the earth beneath it and the heaven above.**'
J. J. Stevenson, *House Architecture*, 1880.

Inhabitants of a small, crowded island, the British have over the last 500 years sheltered themselves in an astonishing variety of dwellings. The design of these homes has been influenced by several factors: the British landscape has, in large part, contributed the building materials, which alter in colour and texture from region to region; changing fashions in architecture and ways of living have transformed house shapes and ornamental features; and developments in technology designed to make living ever more comfortable are often reflected in basic housing forms. Through additions, adaptations, reparations, alterations and demolitions, some British houses are frequently not what they first appear to be, but with further investigation many will reveal themselves.

Most early medieval houses were built with the materials closest to hand, which generally meant timber and mud in various configurations. Around the year 1200, builders began to place timbers on solid foundations, rather than straight into the earth, and thus the lifespan of the buildings was dramatically increased. Timber framework followed several tried and tested forms which tended to differ from region to region. The perishable nature of these materials meant that the shelters built by the majority of the medieval population have not survived, although within the core of many houses there probably still remain beams and masonry from early houses, invisible from the outside and now entirely unrecognisable to the original builder.

From these early periods only the stone buildings of the wealthy have survived. They were principally manors and church foundations where groups of people — lords of the manor, their retinues and servants, monks and nuns, vicars and scholars — lived communally, rather than in individual houses. Monasteries and abbeys had a duty to provide lodgings for travellers: usually set around a courtyard, these rooms formed a protected communal space which remained standard for almshouses, colleges and sheltered housing. Stone was also used

01 Detached 'moderne' house with pantiles and suntrap windows, c. 1930. Dursley, Gloucestershire.

02 Timber-frame Wealden Clergy House; Alfriston, Sussex; 14C.

03 Stone Priest's House; Muchelney, Somerset; 14C and 15C.

for fortifications, defence and as a means of protection (in cellars and vaults) in the houses of merchants and money-lenders. By the end of the 14th century stone was also being used to build relatively small houses, still, however, for the privileged.

The increased wealth and stability of the Tudor period was reflected in an explosion of building. Towns and cities were growing fast and as a result of land enclosure a greater proportion of the population had inheritable landholdings. More people could build more houses and follow the advice offered by Thomas Fuller in the mid-17th century: 'A house had better be too little for a day than too great for a year. And it is easier borrowing from thy neighbour a brace of chambers for the night, than a bag of money for a twelvemonth'. At this point builders of quite ordinary houses began to add extraneous details to create an impression: structural beams were in-filled with purely ornamental patterns, gables decorated, jetties and beams carved. Chimneys were bricked in decorative patterns, and glittering glazed windows of all shapes and sizes completed the picture.

As good timber was a precious resource needed for ship building and the emerging iron industry, vernacular timber-framed houses gradually fell from favour and brick became the principal building material. Not only was a brick house warmer and more stable than a timber one, but bricks were also much more flexible to use. After the Great Fire of London in 1666, a quantity of new legislation was imposed to regulate the rebuilding of the city. Exteriors had to be brick or stone, and height was determined by the width of the street. Standardisation had begun.

Houses are often described as either vernacular or polite: this separates those built in response to materials readily to hand from those built with knowledge of and an eye to new styles, and this usually means Classicism. The first architectural pattern book which introduced Britain to new designs from the Continent was John Shute's *The First and Chief Groundes of Architecture*, published in 1563. These designs were based on the Classical orders and incorporated elements such as friezes, cornices and grotesques. These motifs had come back into fashion during the Italian Renaissance but had been heavily adapted on their journey northwards through France. Appearing first on the façades of the great Elizabethan country houses such as Longleat House and Hardwick Hall, Classical details were in general slow to be absorbed.

However, the Classical influence could be seen in the growing symmetry of house design and the structure of the building. Easier to assimilate were a few stylish motifs: these could be copied from the many books and sheets of engraved architectural ornament that were imported from Germany and the Low Countries (the Netherlands strongly influenced the growing desire for bourgeois comforts). They fused Renaissance elements with Northern Gothic and offered selections of finials, obelisks, heraldic motifs, grotesques heads, strapwork, fruity festoons and triangular pediments which could be carved in wood, stone or even brick, or created in plasterwork to transform old-fashioned timber frames into something more modern.

The Stuart Court too looked to Continental Europe, and specifically to Italy, for the latest taste in art, architecture and literature. Inigo Jones was the main catalyst: he had seen the work of Italian Renaissance architects, in particular Andrea Palladio, at first hand on a journey to Italy in 1613. Jones brought back a copy of Palladio's *Quattro Libri dell'Architettura* and owned drawings by him. While Jones was only working for the most enlightened and wealthy patrons, his vision would, over the next one hundred and fifty years, slowly trickle down to middle- and upper-class Britain, influencing country houses, village houses and town houses for farmers, millers, rectors, manufacturers, naval and army officers, if only in the form of a detail — a door case, window, quoin or string course.

Jones and a few other late 17th- and early 18th-century architects, such as John Webb, Hugh May, Roger Pratt and Lord Burlington, understood how to pull together all the Classical elements in the correct proportions. In place of gables came a straight roof-line and each storey, with its orders, columns, pilasters and string courses, was considered in proportion to the others. The portico and temple front, rusticated basement and ground-floor storeys, balustrading, loggias, pediments, Venetian and Diocletian windows were all new elements which gradually took root as part of the design of British houses. The Civil War and its aftermath delayed the Palladian influence but by the early 18th century it became impossible to build fashionably in any other style.

Classicism was, however, particularly difficult for the average house builder since everyone was aware that rules existed, and there was a palpable fear of making mistakes. Numerous pattern books clearly illustrating examples of the Classical orders (as well as interior

04 Brick town houses; Stoke Newington, London; 1658.

05 Stone town house; Burford, Oxfordshire; 17C.

06 Brick house with pedimented porch; Abinger Hammer, Surrey; c. 1660.

07 Brick house with stone details; Southwell, Nottinghamshire; 1700–20.

08 Cottage in planned village; Milton Abbas, Dorset; 1770s.

09 Stone house in town; Beaminster, Dorset; late 18C.

details such a chimney pieces) were published to inform the client and guide the builder. In addition many earlier houses were re-fronted in the new style, particularly in towns where the inhabitants, increasingly exposed to passing stagecoach travel, might think it commercially sensible to present as contemporary a façade as possible. Isaac Ware, in his lavish and comprehensive book, *The Complete Body of Architecture*, first published in 1756, gives an indication of the pitfalls: 'The proprietor of the intended edifice will have a right to please his fancy in laying out his money, and it is fit he should be indulged, if he chuses it, even at the expense of propriety, in some lesser article, *though not without being informed of it*' (my italics). Ware was keen to establish a standard 'founded upon what a good taste shall most admire in the antique'. A much thinner book, *The Practical Builder or Workman's General Assistant*, published twenty-two years later by William Pain, demonstrates how the audience had widened, as his book was intended 'to furnish the Ignorant, the Uninstructed, with such a comprehensive system of practice, as may lay the foundation for their improvement....'

Pattern books could also provide guidance for those who wished to build more fancifully in the Chinoiserie, Gothick or Rococo styles. Although these exotics were in general more commonly used for interiors and incidental garden buildings, they do manifest themselves as lodges, gateways and other oddities. Tempting illustrations in books such as John Crunden's *The Joyner and Cabinet-maker's Darling or Pocket Director* (1760) and *The Carpenter's Companion, containing 32 New and Beautiful Designs for all sorts of Chinese Railings and Gates* (1765) demonstrated Chinoiserie and Gothick fretwork patterns used, for example, on glazing bars; or Batty Langley's *Ancient Architecture Restored and Improved* (1742) which illustrated crockets, pinnacles, quatrefoil openings, castellated parapets and ogee arches, fed enthusiasts of the Gothick style.

The growing sophistication of town life in the 18th century as centres of commerce and manufacturing, with amusements such as concerts, theatres and assemblies, made towns and cities more comfortable and desirable places to live. Land ownership was increasingly consolidated and landowners planned lucrative developments in the form of planned streets and squares which replaced older, ad hoc town patterns. Classically fronted terraces of uniformly designed houses appeared, their elegant exteriors presenting clean

lines in a relatively small space. As well as work on large houses the Adam Brothers contributed much to the style of terrace building in both London and Edinburgh, and the name Adam (the work of Robert and James with their brother John) became synonymous with certain changes in architectural style from the middle of the 18th century onwards. The inspiration for these changes came directly from new engravings made from Classical Graeco-Roman work drawn on the spot in, for example, Pompeii and Herculaneum. As before, the earliest, rarest and most expensive publications were eventually supplemented by more workaday versions for builders and craftsmen: for example Stephen Riou's *The Grecian Orders* of 1768 offered a digestible form of James Stuart and Nicholas Revett's meticulous study, *Antiquities of Athens* (1762; 2nd vol. 1789). The ornamental motifs that became so fashionable during the second half of the century (anthemions, urns and vases, fluted paterae, honeysuckle, cameos, palmettes, acanthus scrolls, garlands, ram's heads, gryphons and reeding) were therefore not necessarily originally designed for architecture, but came from objects as diverse as Greek vases, Pompeian wall paintings and engraved gems, etc. Applied to features such as exterior ironwork and Coade stone, their style was lighter and airier than Renaissance Classicism: bricks took on paler colours (creams, pale browns, greys and a slightly glossy vitrified blue); windows were larger; the heavy architectural framing of doors and windows disappeared in favour of plainer arched openings with fanlights. These were boom years for speculative terrace building, so much so that a series of Building Acts were introduced to prevent some of the worst excesses of bad practice. These significantly defined how façades should appear: for example the 1774 Act controlled the amount of wood allowed on an exterior.

The style described as Regency corresponds with the period of George IV's influence as a trend-setter, from the early 1780s, when he was Prince of Wales and George III was intermittently incapable of ruling, up to the end of his reign as king in 1830. The prevailing style was largely Classical, but drew on an increasingly eclectic range of sources for its decorative details. There were Egyptian elements in the form of the odd sphinx, obelisk, or lotus capital, given a boost by Nelson's victory over Napoleon at the Battle of the Nile in 1798; conversely, French Empire style (acceptable after the Peace of 1815) contributed some of the ornamentation

10 Stone town houses, terrace; Edinburgh; early 19C.

11 Stucco villa with Gothick details; Sidmouth, Devon; c.1815–20.

12 Stucco house in Italianate style, Camden, London; c. 1840.

beloved of Napoleon's designers: laurel wreaths, eagles, triumphal Classical figures of Fame and Victory, and most popularly Greek Neo-classicism (key patterns, acroteria, thin incised lines, Ionic and Doric columns).

In marked contrast the picturesque ideal created a vision which, in its purest form attempted to evoke wild and untamed nature, and thus create a romantic landscape. This concept, which remained popular well up to the second half of the 19th century, greatly influenced the design of small incidental houses or picturesque village groupings (*cottages ornés*) that could be dropped into the landscape. Although some landowners were undoubtedly aiming to beautify their estates (and house their workers) Charles Middleton in his 1793 pattern book, *Picturesque Views for Cottages, Farm Houses and Country Villas* (one of many on the subject), suggests that potential clients might also be nobility from town who were seeking a temporary retreat: 'Wealthy citizens and persons in official stations, which cannot be far removed from the capital; and ... the smaller kind of provincial edifices, considered either as hunting seats, or habitations of country gentlemen of moderate fortune'.

There was no shortage of designs to choose from. P. F. Robinson's *Village Architecture* even included a workhouse in the guise of an Elizabethan timber-frame mansion. Picturesque details were usually appropriated from the vernacular (at this point often called 'Old English') and exaggerated for effect: fancy thatching, elaborately carved bargeboards, random stonework, irregularly shaped windows, finials, pendants, varied glazing patterns on windows and twisted and patterned chimneys. Rustic work, with rough unsawn timber lending a distinct feel of early 19th-century do-it-yourself, remained a favourite element in this style for many years, even if only in the form of a porch or veranda on a plain cottage. At the same time there was a strand of enthusiasm for what could be loosely termed 'oriental', sometimes waveringly named Hindoo, Turkish, Moorish, Chinese or Saracenic. Similarly, wooden fretwork bargeboards, balconies and window edgings were described as Swiss, Norwegian or Polish. This eclectic range of possibilities remained most popular for incidental garden buildings or a small gardener's cottage.

The speed of construction was increasing and technological advances facilitated the production of cheap and fashionable ornamentation. Improved and expanded cast ironworks (for example,

Wilkinson's 'cupola' blast furnace method of 1794) created not only greater beam strength and an airier, bolder style of building with greater spans than wooden beams would permit, but also enabled a plethora of cheap ironwork features. Improvements in glass manufacture resulted in larger windows and conservatories. By harnessing steam power to woodworking machines Samuel Bentham made fancy mouldings more available. Stuccos, renders and cements that did not fall off meant that uniform walling could be created quickly to cover up cheap building materials. Manufacture provided vastly more choice for the house builder, in an increasingly large market for middle-class housing. Unsurprisingly one of the most influential monthly periodicals, running from 1809 to 1828, was called *The Repository of Arts, Literature, Commerce, Manufacture, Fashions and Politics*. Linked to this expanding market is the first appearance of the estate agent. Early examples in 1822 were Robert Dymond, land surveyor, and Mr. O. Macdonald Jr., from Exeter, who respectfully informed 'the Nobility, Gentry, Land-Surveyors and Builders who have house to let or sell, that ...he is induced to establish an office for that purpose'.

During the late Regency and early Victorian period large-scale terrace developments continued, although greater numbers of crescents and circuses provided more variety, and attempts were often made to widen houses and allow more air into their design. The square, boxy, often semi-detached villa model became highly desirable. Improvements in transport allowed for 'genteel' housing, removed from the town centres. Railways quickly had an impact, as one Victorian (the owner of Basildon Park in Berkshire) wrote: 'We soon shall not want a town house ...all the best physicians will recommend a ride in a steam carriage before dinner as much better than a ride in the park. Cards will read "train off at 6, dinner on table at 7".'

While much building in the country held on to a vaguely picturesque theme there was a more serious and urban alternative in a style developed from the heavy palaces of the Italian Renaissance. Its gravitas was well suited to important civic buildings, gentleman's clubs and libraries and translated easily to housing developments such as Thomas Cubitt's Belgravia in London. Uniform in material (all in stone, or all stuccoed) these houses were heavily rusticated, with large-scale, fat balustrades, sporting guilloche patterns and volutes. There was also a lighter more frivolous version, taking its inspiration

13 Gothic Revival brick house with stone dressings; near Hungerford, Berkshire; 1856.

14 Brick house; Charfield,
Gloucestershire; c. 1885.

15 Brick and terra-cotta villa; Hove,
Sussex; c. 1880–90.

not from Florentine palaces, but from Italian rural houses, and often dubbed 'Tuscan' or 'Italianate'. With wide eaves, bracketed cornices, arched windows and the occasional small 'tower' effect, this style of house was eminently suitable for villas on the edge of towns and new residential areas. Domestic, practical, but not too grand, it became ubiquitous. This was the style that Victoria and Albert chose for Osborne, their substantial holiday house on the Isle of Wight, and it is the style that fronts the sea on many seaside terraces built during this period.

Famously, it was Charles Barry and A. W. N. Pugin's Gothic Revival design that was chosen for the new Houses of Parliament in 1836, and which launched the Gothic Revival's popularity. This was a serious style which, by linking medieval Gothic with Christianity, was used to convey all that was worthy and worthwhile. G. G. Scott and William Butterfield, the leading exponents of the style, agonised over the finer points of authentic decoration for the many new churches they were commissioned to build. The thorough observation of genuine Gothic examples also provided models for details such as elaborate ironwork door hinges and foliage for the 'capitals' on the ubiquitous bay windows of Victorian terraces. Their deliberations resulted in an all-purpose Gothic style for additional parish requirements such as parsonages, almshouses, schools and schoolteachers' houses. The asymmetry of the Gothic Revival style on the exterior was usefully reflected on the interior with rooms of varying sizes and shapes; the pointed arch translated easily onto ordinary British housing. There was also a surge of enthusiasm for colour: polychrome effects with banding and patterning of different coloured bricks was prompted by a burgeoning brick industry, and ceramic encaustic tiles, in imitation of medieval flooring, provided front steps and paths which complemented the exterior style. Complex roof silhouettes were a typical feature of Gothic Revival, with gables and steep pitches, dormer windows, turrets and ornamentation such as patterned roof-ridge tiles and cast-iron crocketed pinnacles. Typical examples built during the 1860s included new houses in North Oxford (with its population suitably composed of churchmen and university dons), the model housing built by textile manufacturer Edward Ackroyd at Ackroydon near Halifax, (for the 'Labouring, Industrial or Artisan Classes') or Leeds Model Cottage Society at Armley. The latter was one of the early responses to the irredeemably appalling and

overcrowded housing conditions that existed for the working classes, particularly in industrial areas. As a contemporary commented on housing in Bradford: 'You think you have been lodged with the Devil incarnate'. The fight for reasonable housing was a major battle over the next seventy years and many philanthropic organisations built block dwellings, lodging-houses and cottage flats in an attempt to ameliorate the situation.

During the latter half of the 19th century miles and miles of terrace housing continued to be built in and around every town and city, often differentiated from its neighbour only by the name over the door. In 1892 George and Weedon Grossmith's *The Diary of a Nobody* began: 'My dear wife Carrie and I have just been a week in our new house The Laurels, Brickfield Terrace, Holloway — a nice six-roomed residence, not counting the basement...'. But land in cities and town centres was in short supply and life in them was noisy, unhealthy and dirty, so for the middle classes the appeal of a new house in the suburbs was considerable.

Suburbs were a buffer zone between town and country. Essentially residential, the inhabitants depended on the city for their living and never really embraced a rural way of life. Speculative builders created suburban Avenues, Parks, Groves and Drives that snaked their way into the countryside, but were still within easy walking distance of electric trams, underground trains and suburban rail links. The Public Health Acts of 1875 meant that some existing housing stock was condemned, and cheap suburban housing designed for letting was also built. Since it adhered to the minimum standards laid down by the Act, it was referred to as 'by-law housing'. To solve the problem of being further away from employment, railway companies ran special workmen's trains (with early hours and very cheap tickets) to and from these areas.

Taste-makers of the subsequent generation looked for an escape from the worthy Gothic Revival and ponderous Renaissance styles. An influential group led by architects Richard Norman Shaw and William Eden Nesfield worked in what was termed at the time the Queen Anne style. This was the form chosen for a new kind of housing, a suburb, an early example of which is Bedford Park in West London, begun in 1875. Abandoning the terrace, its roads curved and twisted. There were trees along the streets, and the houses were individually designed and basementless. The inhabitants walked

16 Rendered house; Wells, Somerset; 1889.

17 Stone house with Art Nouveau cast-iron veranda; Llanbedrog, Gwynedd; c. 1900.

18 Arts and Crafts house; Hampstead Garden Suburb, London; c. 1900.

19 Neo-Georgian house; Hampstead Garden Suburb, London; c. 1910.

through their front gardens and out of their front gate on their journey to the city centre by public transport. Bedford Park was a self-consciously 'artistic' suburb with a community art school and tennis club. The Queen Anne style was also the preferred choice for a number of artists' houses and studios in areas such as Hampstead and Kensington, and could be adapted to the height of mansion flats. Red brick was the prime building material, contrasting with the white-painted wooden windows, small-paned sash and tripartite Venetian windows, door cases with shell-headed canopies, cornices, door cases and wooden balustrading. Ornament appeared in cut and rubbed brickwork, and sunflowers and incidental Japanese-inspired motifs reached epidemic proportions during the 1880s.

The architectural style that had most influence on suburban housing derived from a revolt against the mass-produced aspect of building materials, known as the Arts and Crafts movement. This was apt since twenty years earlier William Morris had moved his family out to the country from where he could commute by train to Morris & Co. in Bloomsbury. Like thousands of tradesman, small businessmen and shopkeepers who came after him, he no longer wanted to live above the shop, and in 1859 he built Red House in Bexleyheath to designs by Philip Webb. This was the first real Arts and Crafts house. It had a medieval feel with small-paned windows, deep red-tiled roofs, rich browny-red brick, large plain wooden doors, generous porches, hand-painted tiles and glass.

Urban Victorian life was one of many restrictions and constrictions and the countryside and vernacular architecture became a growing inspiration for many towards the end of the 19th century. Arts and Crafts architects such as Charles Voysey and M. Hugh Baillie Scott particularly admired tile-hanging, wooden mouldings and cornices, planked doors with latches and strap hinges, weathered oak, oriel windows, leaded casement windows, large generous chimneys and roughcast render — wholly British details that they had seen in Kent and Sussex in particular. They appropriated several of these features for their own buildings, and many of the most popular ones remained part of the standard vocabulary of everyday housing for much of the 20th century.

Houses inspired by Arts and Crafts ideas were a natural fit for new lines in housing such as Lord Lever's village for his workers at Port Sunlight on the Wirral, begun in 1888. Designed by several architects

the houses at Port Sunlight displayed a wide variety of ornament, material and decorative features. There was space and air, greenery, trees, schools, halls and eventually an art gallery. At the same time the social reformer Ebenezer Howard was working on his Garden City Movement. He planned a careful apportioning of land for houses in relation to land for factories while agriculture, smallholdings, fruit farms and forests surrounded the city with a green belt. Raymond Unwin and R. Barry Parker designed the houses for the first Garden City at Letchworth, where building started in 1904.

The 1890 Housing of the Working Classes Act allowed local councils to compulsorily purchase land for housing. The London County Council built central high-density flats, most famously examples at Millbank and in Shoreditch in 1900, which greatly improved on earlier bleak block dwellings. Further out cottage estates appeared — short terraces of cottages with front and back gardens, bordering green spaces. The more idealistic Hampstead Garden Suburb, which was established in 1906 through the efforts of the indomitable Henrietta Barnett, was a community intended for a range of classes from working to upper middle, and even provided flats for independent working women. All houses, cottages and flats had access to a garden.

During the early years of the 20th century a rather more formal Neo-Georgian style presented an alternative to the Arts and Crafts movement. Edwin Lutyens was a leading exponent, influencing many tidy, four-square houses with an emphasis once again on central doorways, sash windows, cornices and quoins. By now magazines had replaced pattern books as disseminators of style. The Builder, first published in 1843, began with detailed line-engravings of current work; Country Life in 1895 printed impeccable photographs of houses old and new. These precursors were followed by an increasingly bulging magazine rack of titles: *Homes and Gardens* (1919), *House and Garden* (1920) and *Ideal Home 'A Monthly Magazine for Home-Lovers'* (1920), which regularly published ground plans and drawings 'designed by Ideal Home' with such headings as 'A Very Comfortable House' and 'A Convenient Bungalow'.

When, during the 1918 election, Prime Minister Lloyd George made rash promises of 'homes fit for heroes', the government was forced to assume the extremely problematic obligation of providing working-class housing. Shortages of labour, money and material were

20 Pebbledash house; Cam, Gloucestershire; 1935.

21 Crittall factory village house;
Silver End, Essex; 1926.

acute after the First World War and much was made of the need for the smaller house. *House and Garden* in 1921 stated that 'except those whom new wealth has made arrogant, or on who ancient birth has laid the burden of keeping up an entailed "seat", everyone was destined to live in small houses'. 'The old ample scale' and the 'large house party' were things of the past. A collection of designs published in 1924 by the Architectural Press put it bluntly: 'We have been faced with the old problem, how to make bricks without straw; and eventually have been driven, bitterly against our will, to consider essentials only, and to rule out every kind of trimming'.

For the middle classes, apart from the economy of maintaining and living in a smaller house, it was no longer possible to count on employing servants. This removed the necessity for the complex warren of back rooms, doors and entrances from which servants operated, and greatly simplified house design. Although coach houses and mews had been eliminated from most house designs by the 1870s, a garage for the car was a frequently consideration by the 1920s, and increasingly added to the specification, being built, as the gate lodge before it, to match the house in architectural detail. It was pointed out (by Lawrence Weaver) in 1910 that unlike the stables, which needed to be well apart from the house for reasons of smell, the 'motor-house' could be included under the main roof, and added 'greatly to the scale and importance of the building without any countervailing disadvantages'. Weaver was rather ahead of his time in his suggestion, since integral garages did not really become popular until the mid-20th century. But by the end of the century, house builders had to think in terms of two- or three-car garages, and once again they became separate buildings.

Growth in road traffic resulted in schemes for new roads and by-passes which became obvious sites for new housing, and remained so until the Ribbon Development Act of 1935 was passed to prevent further encroachment into the countryside. For the vast suburban growth of the inter-war years, which had begun in earnest by the mid-1920s, the generality of housing continued to be built in a well-rehearsed combination of the vaguely vernacular (gable, bay or bow window with leaded lights, tile-hanging or half-timbering). Lack of planning controls had allowed temporary holiday housing to spread in areas of natural beauty producing the reviled 'bungaloid growth' — the 'octopus', as Clough Williams-Ellis called it. Britain's love affair with the rural retreat had suddenly turned sour as more and more cliffs, riversides and hilltops were covered with depressingly uniform Peacehaven-type bungalows called, typically, 'Mon Desire'.

As mortgages became easily available people could buy rather than rent their houses and on purchase they gained the freedom to do with them what they liked (by the 1950s *The Practical Householder*, an early do-it-yourself magazine, had become very popular). A 1936 advertisement for Abbey Road Building Society ran: 'The Slippers on the Hearth — a symbol of perfect domesticity. But there are still many sincere lovers of home whose only disquiet is the knowledge that their home belongs to another. The Building Society movement enables men of modest means to enjoy life not merely as householders but as home-owners'. Hermann Muthesius, commenting in 1904 on the English and their houses, observed: 'The great store that the English still set by owning their home is part of this powerful sense of the English personality. The Englishman sees the whole of life embodied in his house. Here in the heart of his family, self-sufficient and feeling no great urge for sociability, pursuing his own interests in virtual isolation, he finds his happiness and real spiritual comfort'.

By the end of the 1920s the influence of the Modern Movement — the antithesis of mainstream British tradition — was beginning to make an impact. For European architects such as Le Corbusier and the Bauhaus group functionalism was the key, and this was expressed in geometric forms and concrete surfaces, glass and steel. Roofs were flat, and curves were circular or semi-circular. Elements such as copings, cornices and string mouldings were eradicated and ornament was minimal, with just the occasional suggestion of streamlining through parallel vertical banding. Such houses were mainly painted white, a startling look in many British environments: as Lionel Brett wrote in 1947 there was a faction for whom 'a white wall was a red rag, and a flat roof a badge of bolshevism'.

Very few houses were built in the pure Modern Movement style, but a watered-down British version was popular in the early 1930s and generally termed by builders 'moderne'. It was an appropriately unconventional style for flats that were perceived as an uncompromisingly modern type of housing for Britain. Favourite features were 'suntrap' windows, balconies, and flat roofs with a smattering of Art Deco motifs such as chevrons, sunrays and ziggurat shapes. Concrete, though fashionable, was not a material that the

22 Brick and cladding house; Clacton-on-Sea, Essex; 1960s.

23 House with flat roof and picture windows; Highgate, London; 1960s.

24 Brick house in countryside; Happisburgh, Norfolk; late 18C/ early 19C.

25 Brick house in development; Shepton Mallet, Somerset; 1998.

average builder found easy to use (it cracked and often became streaky). Thus, until the outbreak of the Second World War, many houses continued to be built in brick, or brick rendered with white-painted cement to give the same effect.

So much housing was bombed during the war that the government set up a Temporary Housing Programme in 1944 with the result that by the following year the first prefabs (pre-fabricated bungalows) were erected on derelict sites, vacant land and parks to house the homeless. Ingeniously compact and set within little gardens they were made principally from steel, timber, concrete and asbestos cement sheet. A later type was made by the aircraft industry in aluminium — a post-war switch from bombers to bungalows. Housing shortages led to 'conversions': in such conditions people lived in railway carriages, shepherds' huts and even double-decker buses. But during the 1950s many permanent homes were created from mews, coach houses, windmills and farm buildings and numerous large houses were split into flats. This was the beginning of an important trend which, by the late 20th century, encompassed warehouses, factories and even office blocks. Pre-fabricated concrete sections were used during the 1950s for some local authority housing, for example at Hartcliffe estate in Bristol for two-storey houses and 'walk-up' flats.

Part of the national post-war plan was the creation of New Towns to be built in the countryside (first Harlow and Stevenage begun in the 1950s, followed by towns such as Peterlee, Cumbernauld and Milton Keynes a decade later) and green belts around cities. In the period of post-war austerity and shortages, the houses, terraces and low- rise flats aimed to be strictly functional with the minimum of extraneous elements. A pared-down functional style created with available materials, particularly in public housing, meant that choices were limited: steel tubing might be used for porch supports or front gates; glass bricks for providing hall light beside front doors; render over brick for an alternative finish. Many of the typical designs of the 1950s and the 1960s involved a theme of panels and framing, colours and texture. In ornament the fashion was for the abstract, rather than anything that derived from past civilisations. The architecture devised for the Festival of Britain popularised a range of geometric shapes — lozenges, hexagons and spheres deriving from scientific models —

and these appeared as panel shapes, or in metalwork. Plain windows were surrounded with a frame, and panels of cladding (developed from the technique of pre-fabrication) provided colour and texture using new technological developments in plastics and glass.

Driven by the political need to provide housing quickly, high-density tower blocks were seen as one solution. Quick system building could deliver modern living spaces. As the architect Frederick Gibberd said in 1955, high blocks gave 'more pleasure to more people...a new kind of space, surprise views'. The novelty of height, previously associated only with luxury flats and hotels, was made available to all. Cities in the sky were to replace the miles of outworn, outmoded Victorian terraces that architects and planners were quick to denounce as slums. Functionalism was the keyword and seemingly endless horizontals and verticals dominated the design of over four million public dwellings that were built between 1945 and the end of the 1960s.

At the end of the 20th century the pressure grew to revolutionise house-building: to produce houses with a low environmental impact by incorporating the latest technology in energy-saving features and by using sustainable or recycled building materials. This has also led to a re-evaluation of vernacular architecture. While this initiative has produced new designs and forms, for most British people their love affair with the brick box seems destined to last forever. There, in the unending combinations of architectural structure and ornamentation, the British passion for personalising their homes has created one of the strongest links between the Britain of today and the last 500 years of a small, crowded island's history.

26 Underground house on coastal headland; Pembrokeshire; 1997.

27 Housing association terrace; Greenwich Millennium Village, London; 2000.

Apartments, Flats and Tenements

Horizontal apartment living was adopted by the Scots from the 17th century onwards, but resisted by the English until the very late 19th century. Lifts were key to making multi-storey living a desirable option. Hydraulic lifts were introduced in 1882, but subsequently they were powered by electricity.

Apartments, Flats and Tenements

The English and Welsh, until recently, have never been enthusiastic about flats. In 1911 only about three per cent of the housing stock were flats, unlike in Continental Europe where apartments have always been the city-living norm. Scotland, however, has been the exception; Edinburgh's constricted geography meant that from the 16th century houses were built with eight or nine storeys which were divided horizontally and known as tenements, a term for a dwelling that is rented or 'held' rather than owned. The wealthiest lived at the top, farthest away from the stink of the street, but linked by a common stair, with the most inferior quarters at ground level. 'Flat' was the Scottish term for 'storey', and hence the term was coined. Even when Edinburgh spread to the New Town in the 18th century a proportion of the terrace houses was divided into flats for middle-class occupation and these remained the most frequent form of housing until the 20th century. Glasgow in particular was renowned for its tenements, but their descent into 20th-century slums gave them unsavoury reputations.

Victorian housing reformers and charitable trusts such as Peabody built multi-storey blocks as habitable dwellings for the working class in city centres where the workforce was needed. Industrial building techniques such as cast-iron structures, fireproofing and external staircases were adapted for domestic use. In 1865 the City of London built what were in effect the first council houses: Corporation Buildings on Farringdon Road was six storeys high with rooms for 168 families. In his novel *The Nether World* (1889) George Gissing describes a similar block as 'barracks, in truth; housing for the army of industrialism'. Named 'Blocks', 'Buildings' and 'Dwellings' flats were more often associated with the poor; called 'Mansions' the middle classes began to see them as desirable. One of the earliest, Albert Hall Mansions by R. Norman Shaw built in 1880–87, had six storeys, a hydraulic lift, bathrooms and wine cellars.

28 Red brick mansion blocks completed in 1903 in a residential area developed by the Paddington Trustees and the Church Commissioners. It is typical of a number of similar red-brick mansion blocks built from 1897 to 1907 along wide tree-lined avenues in that area, differing slightly in the detail: disposition of balconies, fenestration and entrance ornamentation. Biddulph Mansions, Maida Vale, West London.

29 Two tenement buildings dating from the late 15C and mid 16C and restored in 1916. Rendered in harling, the staircase lies within the turreted section. Abbey Strand, Royal Mile, Edinburgh.

In 1880 the architectural writer J.J. Stevenson described the 'system to which the name of "mansions" has been given' as like hotels with the convenience of being able to come and go at will, of being freed from the tyranny of servants and housekeeping, with public rooms and a central kitchen. The problem of making and receiving calls with only a communal entrance was solved by the presence of a porter or a 'speaking-tube'. Lavish decoration in the form of terra-cotta ornament and elaborate ironwork marked them as superior housing.

After World War I the popularity of flats increased. With the shortage of both housing and domestic servants they also suited the increasing number of women living independent lives. New ways of building with steel frame and reinforced concrete simplified the construction of large structures, and electricity delivered heat and light cleanly. It is characteristic of the period that Devonshire House, an eight-storey block on Piccadilly, could be built on the site of the

30 Block of sandstone tenements, dating from c. 1900. As in a modern block of flats the windows are of the same dimensions at every storey. West End, Glasgow.

31 Model lodging house built by the Brewer's Company for working men in the trade. Designed by E.H. Martineau in 1871–72 it appears to have been ten years in the building since one door is dated 1882. Unusually decorative for this type of building the block is patterned with polychrome brick. Brewery Buildings, Clerkenwell, London.

32 Built round a quadrangle of limewashed render in the Arts and Crafts style and designed by M.H. Baillie Scott in 1908, this block provided fifty flats specifically for independent working women and was the brainchild of Dame Henrietta Barnett. Waterlow Court, Hampstead Garden Suburb, North London.

single palatial town house of the Duke of Devonshire in 1926. The modernity and luxury of the enterprise was frequently expressed by up-to-the-minute Art Deco features. Initially it was intended that the flats, whatever size the block was, would be self-contained communities as pioneered by Le Corbusier: the small block of flats in the Isokon Building in Hampstead had a laundry, shoe-shining and communal kitchen facilities; and the massive Dolphin Square, built slightly later in 1935–37, boasted 1,250 flats, shops, swimming pool and croquet lawn. Reliable lifts coupled with the technique of pouring concrete on-site allowed for much taller buildings, and during the 1950s and 1960s tower blocks twenty to thirty storeys high were seen by local authorities as an economic solution to housing shortages. The 1970s and 1980s saw many blocks falling into disrepair and disfavour, but the form has gradually revived in popularity. Reinvented and improved as 'apartment buildings' (now considered a positive term), flats today are often a perfect home for smaller-sized households.

30		34
31		35
32	33	36

33 Detail of one of five blocks of flats in a self-contained enclave, complete with lodge, swimming pool and club room, built 1934–36 by R. Toms & Partners. The showy architectural detail of Cape Dutch gables and Spanish-inspired balconies could have been influenced by the nearby Ealing Film Studios completed nearby a few years earlier. Ealing Village, West London.

34 At the time of building this complex of luxury flats, designed by architect Gordon Jeeves, was described as the largest self-contained block in Europe. It consists of 13 brick 'houses' with minimal exterior features placed around the inner central square with over 1,200 flats. Dolphin Square, Pimlico, London

35 Block of apartments beside the river Thames, built in 1983 and designed by Nicholas Lacey. Its crescent form allows for each module of housing to be cantilevered out one above the other, and gives uninterrupted views up and down the river. Crown Reach, London.

36 Cluster tower block of flats designed by Denys Lasdun as public housing and completed in 1960 but refurbished in 2001 as private apartments. There are four slim blocks each 16 storeys high, angled to allow each flat an uninterrupted view outward from one façade. They are built around a central staircase and lift which avoids long access balconies. Keeling House, Bethnal Green, East London.

Balconies and Verandas

37 Iron balconies and canopies on terrace; Cheltenham, Gloucestershire; c. 1815–20.

38 Iron balcony with palmette motif; Adam Street, London; c. 1768.

39 Continuous balcony along terrace; New Town, Edinburgh; 1820s.

A stone balustrade cantilevered out from a first-floor window was a typically Classical form that appeared occasionally on grand houses in the 17th century. This style was more associated with fashion than utility since balconies were rarely a natural choice in the British climate. Hermann Muthesius described them as 'lifeless appendages', considering the bay window to be the British alternative. Nevertheless, from the 1770s onwards, ironwork balconies became almost ubiquitous on terrace housing. They were designed either as single balconies fronting first-floor windows (and providing a safety guard), or ran continuously along the terrace providing both a practical fire escape and a place for a few plants.

Balconies, along with verandas (the same motif but at ground level) were a key feature of Regency style, and both frequently featured a scallop-edged canopy of copper or zinc. A canopied balcony of this period is often referred to as a Trafalgar balcony. This was also the moment when the British discovered the seaside and the sea-view, and indeed balconies have remained an essential part of British seaside architecture. Balconies were most in demand for flat-dwellers and were usually incorporated into the design of both mansion flats and artisan blocks. They were a space to take the air, grow a few plants (Victorian garden literature contains many references to 'window gardening'), and a convenient place to dry washing in the absence of a communal drying green or garden.

At the turn of the 20th century sleeping outside was considered highly desirable, and some houses in garden cities and suburbs were designed with 'sleeping balconies'. Capitalising on the benefits of maximum sun and air was a central tenet of the Modern Movement and as much balcony space, roof terrace and open-air walkways were incorporated into flat design as possible. The veranda on a bungalow was equally designed to encourage outdoor living.

37	40	41	
38	42	43	44
39	45		

40 Iron balconies and canopies facing the sea; Royal Crescent, Brighton, Sussex; 1798–1807.

41 Canopied iron balcony; Holborn, London; c. 1805–10.

42 Canopied iron balcony on bow-fronted house; Bath; c. 1810.

43 Iron veranda; Pwllheli, Gwynedd; c.1820.

44 Canopied iron balcony on bow-fronted house; Brighton, Sussex; c. 1820–25.

45 Continuous iron balcony across terrace façade; Bath; c. 1810.

Balconies and Verandas

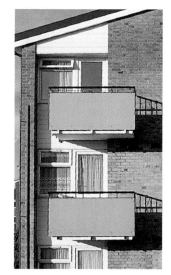

46 Iron balconies on model dwellings; Shoreditch, London; 1860–62.

47 Concrete and steel balconies on walk-up block of flats; Stevenage New Town, Hertfordshire; 1955–57.

48 Wooden balconies with metal struts on self-build terrace; Lewisham, London; 1970s.

49 Iron balconies on mansion flats; Westminster, London; c. 1890.

50 Stone and iron balconies on flats; Kensington, London; 1898.

51 Iron and wood balcony off bedroom; Cardiff; c. 1900.

52 Brick and concrete balconies on flats; Ealing, London; c. 1935.

46	47 48	53 54
49 50 51 52		55 56 57 58

53 Balconies on Trellick Tower, built as public housing; Notting Hill, London; 1973.

54 Brick balconies on flats; Chelsea, London; 1952.

55 Concrete balconies on Highpoint, Modern Movement block of flats; Highgate, London; 1936–38.

56 Glass and brick balconies on flats; St John's Wood, London; late 1960s/early 1970s.

57 Slatted wood balconies and walkways; Byker Wall, Newcastle-on-Tyne; 1970s.

58 Metal balcony on BedZED, carbon neutral housing development; Sutton, Surrey; 2002.

Bargeboards

Also sometimes referred to as vergeboards, bargeboards are wooden planks fixed to gable and eave with the original purpose of providing protection against the weather. Original bargeboards appeared only on timber-frame houses (never stone) and examples with cusped and scalloped decorative edging are extant from the mid-14th century. A prime area for decorative carving, bargeboards became increasingly elaborate particularly by the late 16th century when jetties and multiple gables were the focus of architectural style. Gothic motifs, such as quatrefoils and trefoils, were pierced through the boards and elaborate finials and pendants were added at the apex and eave.

Bargeboards re-emerged as part of the picturesque, 'Old English', Tudor, Elizabethan and Gothic Revivals. No longer part of a timber-frame structure bargeboards also appeared on stone, brick and rendered houses, and the shadow cast by the patterned board on the wall became an important decorative element. Since they are wood and liable to deteriorate bargeboards were often replaced, and some later Victorian replacements were very wide and elaborately carved. They were also added to plain houses to give them an instant picturesque appeal.

Simpler, thinner (and thus more economic) bargeboards feature on Edwardian terraces and suburban houses, frequently in conjunction with mock half-timbering.

59 Timber-frame cottage with original cusped bargeboard; Steventon, Oxfordshire; 14C.

60 Running scroll pattern; Long Melford, Suffolk; 17C.

59	61 62	63
60	64 65 66	67

61 Scrolling vine pattern; Halstead, Essex; later addition to 17C pub.

62 Acorns and oak leaves; Kingsbridge, Devon; c. 1840.

63 Zig-zag pattern on estate cottages; Badminton, Gloucestershire; 1860.

64 Trefoils and cusping on gate lodge; Greenwich, London; mid-19C.

65 Tudor Revival trefoils and cusping; Chester, Cheshire; mid-19C.

66 Quatrefoils, finial and pendant on Holly Village estate cottage; Highgate, London; 1865.

67 Festoon pattern on terrace; Bridgewater, Somerset; c. 1880.

Boundaries

The house-dweller can immediately engender a sense of security by encircling the plot to create a defensible space, and this boundary is often the detail which best expresses how the inhabitant wishes to be viewed by the outside world. A 14th-century cottage in Chaucer's *Nun's Priest's Tale* was 'enclosed al aboute with stikkes, and a drye dych without', suggesting that the desire to fortify even insignificant houses has a long history.

The gatehouse or lodge is an extension of this desire in its implication that someone is permanently guarding the entrance. For the most part, however, people have had to content themselves with a gate and a wall, fence or hedge. For aristocrats, carved stone heraldic crests perched on gate piers symbolised a watchful presence, for others a range of balls, cones, urns, eagles and pineapples (signifying hospitality and welcome) were used. In 1756 Isaac Ware wrote that a niche was an essential part of a gate pier in order to provide a seat for the weary visitor arriving by foot 'to take in refreshment and the prospect'. In the 18th century the grandest gates were usually of wrought iron, and even terrace houses sometimes emphasised their entrances with iron overthrows (arches which usually incorporated a lamp). In the interests of uniformity, gates and railings were supplied by the builder along the length of the terrace, while individual choice was restricted to detached houses.

By the end of the 19th century there was a revival of interest in hedges, wooden gates and picket fences. For example hedges were specified for Hampstead Garden Suburb as a deliberate move against urban iron or cheap walling made from clinker. A late 20th-century enthusiasm for the almost total privacy afforded by fast-growing cypress leylandii trees led to demands for a law limiting the height of hedge boundaries.

68 Limestone slab fence; Filkins, Oxfordshire.

69 Granite wall with white quartz boulders along top; Newport, Pembrokeshire.

70 Unpainted wooden picket fence; Crofton, Wiltshire.

68	71		
69	72	73	74
70	75	76	77

71 Iron railings; Dedham, Essex; late 19C.

72 Solid iron fencing and gate piers; Clifton, Bristol; c. 1850.

73 Arts and Crafts wooden fencing and gates; Bedford Park, London; 1880s.

74 Cinder wall, wooden lap fence and hedge on terrace housing; Highgate, London; c. 1900.

75 Post and chain; Burnham Market, Norfolk.

76 Random wall made from scrap and rubble; Frinton-on-Sea, Essex.

77 Topiary hedge and bank; East Lambrook, Somerset.

Brick

For centuries Britain lagged behind continental Europe in brick-making, and until the 15th century there are only incidental examples of their use. Techniques of brick-making and brick-laying came from Flanders, Holland and Northern Germany (where there was no stone for building) via close trading links with towns in Eastern England. In 1571 Elizabeth I granted a charter to the Tylers' and Bricklayers' Company, an indication that brick was fast becoming an important building material not only for new buildings but also as a fireproof solution for 'a multitude of chimneys lately erected', as reported by William Harrison in his *Description of England* (1577). Bricks could also strengthen existing timber-frame houses, by replacing the wattle and daub with nogging. The advantages were clear: bricks could usually be made near the site (suitable clay was to be found in much of the country; the clay was dug in autumn and made into bricks in spring); since they were made in moulds bricks came in a variety of convenient sizes, and they were resilient and warmer than stone.

From the outset the decorative possibilities of bricks were fully exploited, as they could be laid in patterns of contrasting colours and combined with other materials such as flint and stone. Bricks were laid in varying 'bonds' or combinations of stretchers (the brick's longest side) with headers (its shortest). The most common was English bond which alternated courses of stretchers and headers. Flemish bond, which became the most popular in the 18th century, alternated stretchers and headers within every course. Stretching bond, since it only used stretchers, made the most economical use of bricks. A labour-intensive technique called tuck pointing (defining the mortar with a thin white line) demonstrated conspicuous expenditure on a façade.

Bricks could be cut or painstakingly rubbed with a piece of grit-stone to make decorative cornices, pilasters, window and door frames. Special soft, smooth red bricks were produced for this gauged brickwork and laid to fit tightly so that the mortar was hardly visible.

78 Brick cottage; Maldon, Essex; 18C.

79 Brick nogging within timber-framing; Aldeburgh, Suffolk; 16C.

80 Cut-brick window surround; Cromwell House, Highgate, London; 1637–40.

78		81	82
79		83	84
80			85

81 Estate cottage with decorative brick and timber-framing; Albury, Surrey; 1850s.

82 Brick bow in red and vitreous brick; Benson, Oxfordshire; late 18C.

83 Red stretchers and blue headers laid in Flemish bond with red gauged brick over window and door; Overton, Hampshire; late 18C/early 19C.

84 Detail of striped red brick and black-glazed brick on semi-detached cottage; Mudford, Somerset; 1860.

85 Red machine brick on suburban house; Cardiff; 1920s.

Brick

86 Tuck pointed brick laid in Flemish bond; Marylebone, London; 18C.

87 Brick laid in English bond, Norfolk, 17C.

88 Brick side wall, showing stucco quoins of façade; Sutton House, Hackney, London; 16C.

89 Brickwork showing lime mortar; Orford, Suffolk; 18C.

90 Diamond of dark, vitreous brick laid amongst red, almshouse; Farnham, Surrey; 1619.

91 Polychrome brickwork in grey, red and white on terrace; Reading, Berkshire; late 19C.

92 Cut and rubbed brick pediment over porch with Renaissance Revival motifs; Hampstead, London; 1890s.

93 Gault brick; Bury St Edmunds, Suffolk; early 19C.

These techniques were highly prized in the 17th century and revived when exposed brickwork was reappraised in the 1850s after decades of stucco.

Originally bricks came in a variety of colours depending on clay and firing, so when brick-making became mechanised at the end of the 19th century the subtle variations of handmade bricks were lost. Fashions in colour also changed. From the late 17th century to the 1730s the style was for red or purple and dark grey with red dressings. Later, browner, greyer more stone-like colours were preferred, which in turn gave way to yellow and cream during the Regency period.

A brick tax that lasted from 1784 until 1850 meant that double duty was levied on large or ornamental bricks. As soon as the tax was repealed Victorian brick-makers produced a wider range of colours and shapes, pressed with patterns and motifs. The production of cheap bricks was made possible in the late 1870s when a seam

of clay with a high carbon content was discovered at Fletton near Peterborough that could be pressed straight into moulds and put through a kiln that burnt continuously. So-called Fletton bricks thus became a by-word for economy. Inspiration for polychrome brickwork came in part from illustrations of Venetian Gothic buildings in John Ruskin's *Stones of Venice* (1851–53). The author later commented: 'I have had an indirect influence on nearly every cheap villa builder between this and Bromley'.

Dark red bricks returned to favour in the 1870s to 1890s only to be condemned in 1906 as a 'scarlet fever' by the Arts and Crafts architect M. Hugh Baillie Scott. With mass production bricks became totally predictable in size, colour and texture. Subsequently, and often in response to the conservation lobby, many companies started to manufacture bricks in a variety of different textures and motley colourings.

86	87	88		92	93	
89	90	91		94	95	96

94 Cream bricks in stretcher bond; Kentish Town, London; 1992.

95 Grey brick walls with red brick quoins, string course and window surrounds; Sulhamstead, Berkshire; 1906–1912.

96 Mottled bricks, public housing; Bristol; 1960s.

Brick Houses

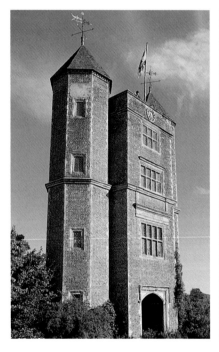

97 Gate tower; Sissinghurst, Kent; 1560s.

98 Classical house with brickwork quoins; Balls Park, Hertford, Hertfordshire; 1643.

99 Terrace; Bridgewater, Somerset; 1720s.

100 Terrace; Islington, London; late 18C.

101 Terrace; Liverpool, Merseyside; late 18C.

102 Terrace of gault brick and flint; Sudbury, Suffolk; early 19C.

103 Polychrome brick cottage; Orford, Suffolk; mid-19C.

104 Brick almshouses, Nantwich, Cheshire; mid-19C.

105 Stone with pale brick; Great Torrington, Devon; 1880s.

97	98	99		101	102	103
		100		104	105	106
				107	108	

106 Terrace of brick with terracotta Gothic decorations; Port Sunlight, Cheshire; 1896.

107 Mottled brick house with waney-edged weatherboard gable; Chelmsford, Essex; 1950s.

108 Brickwork emphasised with white mortar; Hampstead, London; 1930s.

41

Bungalows, Crofts and Single-storey Houses

The simplest and most basic of housing forms, single-storey houses are the most straightforward to build and therefore have the longest history. Their later incarnation as bungalows accentuated the positive: they were convenient, economic, easy to pre-fabricate and extended the pleasure of home-ownership to many who otherwise could not have afforded it.

Bungalows, Crofts and Single-storey Houses

Traditionally, in the wilder and remoter parts of Britain in particular, houses were built as a single storey. It was a cheaper and simpler solution to build long and low, rather than upwards, and this was particularly true when the inhabitant might be building his own home, for example a croft in the Scottish Highlands and Islands. A croft is a particular type of tenancy and refers to the land rented by the crofter, but also describes the dwelling on the land, usually built from local materials.

Bungalow is the usual term for a single-storey house. The word is a westernised pronunciation of the Indian term for 'hut' of the type imitated by the Empire builders of the British Raj: low, sprawling houses shaded by a veranda. The first true British bungalow was built as a holiday house in 1869 at Birchington on the Kent coast. From the start bungalows suggested relaxation and retreat. H. G. Wells's novel *In the Days of the Comet* (1906) describes a bungalow village inhabited by 'artistic-minded and carelessly living people' occupying railway carriages turned into 'habitable little cabins for the summer holiday...improvised homes, gaily painted and with broad verandas and supplementary lean-to's'. The bungalow's lack of middle-class niceties such as a tradesman's entrance or upstairs bedrooms appeared at the time to be distinctly louche. A few architects considered bungalows worthy of attention, notably Robert Briggs who published *Bungalow and Country Residences* in 1891: 'What we mean by a bungalow is an artistic little dwelling, cheaply, but soundly built with a proper regard to sanitation, and popped down in some pretty little spot with just enough accommodation for our particular needs'. It was this wish to place bungalows 'at the seaside or in the country in positions chosen for the quality of the air or for recreative facilities', as P. T. Harrison in *Bungalow Residences* (1909) put it, that attracted the opprobrium of those fighting to preserve the countryside, such as the founders of the Campaign to Protect Rural England in 1926.

109   An early 20C stone bungalow with veranda linking the two bay windows which, like those on the terrace houses further down the hill, have decorative bargeboards. Beechen Cliff, Bath.

110   Two rows of almshouses intended for the poor of the parish. The thatched dwelling was originally the priest's house but was converted in 1589 into four almshouses; the building with the bargeboard was built in 1713 for eight inhabitants, but on restoration in 1975 this was reduced to dwellings for three. Thaxted, Essex.

Many bungalows were built on land unsuitable for permanent development — riversides, shorelines, pockets of farmland — but as they were only intended for holiday use they avoided planning regulations. Typical of these were the communities of Jaywick Sands in Essex and the so-called 'Plotlands' in Essex and Kent. Here east-enders from London travelled out on trains and buses to build their own small rural retreats. When the government was faced with an acute housing shortage towards the end of World War II prefabricated bungalows were the quick-fix solution in a country short of materials and skilled construction workers. Let to families with young children they were intended to have a life span of ten to fifteen years.

Stereotypically the modern bungalow is an appropriate house for retirement and old age as it eliminates problematical staircases. This can be seen as continuation of a pattern set by almshouses, many of which were single storey. The latter were housing for the poor and needy, supported by donations of alms. The earliest existing foundation is the Hospital of St Cross in Winchester, founded for thirteen poor men in 1136. Saving your soul by the establishment of a charitable foundation for housing was a frequent strategy of the wealthy in the late 15th century, a trend which continued well into the 19th century, although latterly almshouses were also endowed by guilds, livery companies or corporations. Many 20th-century sheltered housing schemes also follow the pattern of enclosed quadrangle space common in the design of almshouses.

111 Traditional single-storey croft; the exceptionally thick granite walls are double layered with an infilling of sand and topped with turf, flowers or even occasionally rhubarb. The thatch, which was sea grass from the dunes, was laid on loose and anchored down with rope netting held in place with stones or chicken wire, a precaution against fierce winds. Tiree, Inner Hebrides.

112 A light timber-frame bungalow with the classic veranda probably built in the 1920s. Wellington, Herefordshire.

113 Bungalow romantically named 'Glencoe'; very minimal with two rooms and asbestos tile roof. The careful painting of the brick gives the illusion of quoins. Stedham, Sussex.

114 One of about 80 bungalows and shacks built on shingle ridges on Romney Marsh. Some were erected by fishermen, the others were self-built by workers employed by Southern Railways. Some of them used the company's old rolling stock as a core and gradually extended to make a holiday shack. In the 1960s they were connected to drainage and electricity. Dungeness, Kent.

111			
112		114	115
113		116	117
			118

115 Prefab aluminium bungalow, codenamed B2, which was developed by the Aircraft Industries Research Organisation for Housing from 1945 onwards, and craned onto site with interior fitting complete. Other prefabs, such as the Arcon and Phoenix types were steel or timber framed and clad in asbestos cement panels. Cam, Gloucestershire.

116 Basic bungalow built on farmland in the 1920s with no access to a proper road or utilities but with the views facing south overlooking the estuary, harbour and to the sea beyond. It was the siting of bungalows in beauty spots such as this that caused such outrage. This was demolished in the early 21C and rebuilt to modern specifications. Salcombe, Devon.

117 Although essentially single-storey, some bungalows were designed with a single upstairs room. The craze for sunlight during the 1920s and 1930s led to some bungalows, such as this one, being built on a canted plan to take maximum advantage of the south-facing aspect. It has a modern replacement door and ground-floor windows. Bingley, Yorkshire.

118 County Durham low-rise. A terrace of single-storey houses built by the local authority for the elderly, 1960s. Brandon, Co. Durham.

Ceramics

Until the invention of a frost-proof tile there was little opportunity to use ceramic tiles as exterior decoration, and until they were mass-produced there could be little demand. During the Gothic Revival period, however, there was a renewed interest in medieval flooring tiles (inlaid with patterns of contrasting coloured clays) and the encaustic tile, which was frost-proof, was developed during the 1830s.

The potter, Herbert Minton, was the prime mover in the re-introduction of tiling. Experimenting with techniques as early as 1828, he bought a share in Samuel Wright's patent for mechanical tile production in 1830. Minton also worked closely with the Gothic Revival architect A. W. N. Pugin (who enthusiastically advocated a public statue of Minton holding up a tile), and commercial production got underway. Thinner glazed wall tiles went into production around 1840. Encaustic tiles were popular for paths and doorsteps and occasionally as a decorative frieze on façades around doors or windows. The earliest colours were white and red; by the 1880s buff, brown, black, blue, green and pink had extended the range.

Small, geometrically shaped tiles and tesserae for mosaics were made to accompany the encaustic tiles and widen the scope of their applications. Hygiene was a buzzword of the late 19th century and thus glazed tile porches became extremely popular, being both easy to clean and highly decorative. Many applications of ceramic decoration were commercial, rather than domestic, although occasional examples appear, such as the work done by the sculptor Gilbert Bayes for the St Pancras Housing Association in majolica (tin-glazed earthenware), which enjoyed a revival at the turn of the century. Panels of cladding which produced colour and texture were typical on new building of the 1950s, and tiling was often introduced at this date.

119		122	123
120		124	125
121		126	127

119 Encaustic tiles on front path, steps and porch; Clapham, London; house 1850s, (tiling later).

120 Encaustic tile panel set above front door; Hornsey, London; 1870s.

121 Mosaic doorstep incorporating number of house; Camden, London; 1870s.

122 Tiled porch incorporating dado; Cardiff; c. 1900.

123 Majolica finial on communal washing posts at St Pancras Housing Association flats; Camden, London; 1938.

124 Majolica tympanum to window (depicting Sleeping Beauty) in St Pancras Housing Association flats; Camden; 1938.

125 Glazed brick wall of flats; Bermondsey, London; 1990s.

126 Random coloured tiles as decorative cladding on local authority flats; Camden, London; 1950s.

127 Art Nouveau glazed tiled porch; Bath; c. 1900.

Chimneys

The history of chimney design is derived from the opposing needs to obtain maximum heat on the one hand, while controlling the fire inside the building on the other.

Early dwellings had a hearth in the centre of the living space (or 'hall') and the smoke found its way out of a hole in the roof. The hole (also known as a 'wind eye' from which the word window derives) had a louver arrangement of timber or pottery which created an up-draught. These medieval arrangements are recorded occasionally in poor rural areas of Britain until the 19th century. With thatch and timber-frame construction, fire was a constant hazard and a thatched house, or one that previously was thatched, would frequently have a very high chimney to keep the sparks away from the roof. Unsurprisingly chimneys were common in towns well before the country.

Once houses were built on two storeys the fireplace — and a chimney — had to stand along the wall. Early Norman examples are stone, but it was the increased use of brick in the 16th century that gave a huge impetus to the building of chimneys which became a prestige feature on houses. During that period although it was easier to build chimneys on end-gable walls, to make maximum use of the chimney (and its warmth) it was better to place them centrally, thus providing back-to-back fireplaces for two main rooms. By the middle of the 16th century sophisticated chimney builders could place four flues in one stack. These were built large and tall and their presence was often accentuated with fancy brickwork or by diagonal placement of the chimney. In Scotland wallhead chimneys were placed at the top of gables, rising from the eaves. If the house was built in the Classical style appropriate ornament was sometimes adopted with shaped cornices or rustication.

As the problem of smoking fires persisted, theories of efficient chimney design abounded. The invention of chimney pots (or tops, as they were first called) was a breakthrough as they increased up-

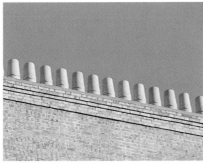

128		131	132
129		133	134
130			

128 Crooked brick chimney; Maldon, Essex; 19C.

129 Lodging for clergy; Vicars' Close, Wells, Somerset; mid-14C with later alterations.

130 Timber-frame farmhouse with brick chimney; High Easter, Essex; 15C/16C.

131 Gate lodge with Elizabethan Revival terracotta chimneys; Highgate, London; c.1850.

132 Chimney pots on Peabody Trust block dwelling; Chelsea, London; 1871.

133 Chimney stacks and pots on stone terrace housing; Bath; late 18C.

134 Cut brick columns on polygonal stack; Blandford Forum, Dorset; c.1660.

Chimneys

135 Brick stacks laid on the diagonal; Godmanchester, Cambridgeshire; 16C.

136 Stone stack; Smithills Hall, Bolton, Lancashire; 16C stack with 19C ceramic pot.

137 Vernacular whitewashed stone stack with wind prevention device; Croggan, Isle of Mull, Argyll and Bute.

138 Tudor Revival moulded terra-cotta pots; Charlton Musgrove, Somerset; c. 1860.

135 136 137 138   143

139 140 141 142   144

draught. They came into general use in the second half of the 18th century, and as a result the shape of the chimney was reduced to just a plinth for the pots. Increasing expectations of home comfort, plus easier transportation of coal, meant that bedrooms, and even attics, were built with fireplaces, and chimney pots proliferated.

The tall chimney stack with smoke curling from the top remained, however, still an essential part of the picturesque rural vision, and the importance of the chimney as an element of house design was reinstated in the early 19th century, particularly on buildings that might be labelled 'Tudor', 'Elizabethan' or 'Old English'. Tall chimneys also reflected the inglenook fireplace in an enlarged hall that was a central feature of the Arts and Crafts house. In the suburbs the gently smoking chimney, along with the lamp-lit window, became an iconic welcoming beacon for the commuter (a contrast to the thousands of smoking chimneys that choked the city air in Gustave Doré's images of London terraces).

Prominent chimneys featured during the 1950s and 1960s on American-influenced ranch-style houses in the form of large buttress-like structures. By contrast central heating, which was first generally adopted in blocks of flats during the inter-war period, became the norm in post-Second World War housing and the chimney was consequently abandoned. After this brief eclipse the chimney returned as a metal flue, and in retro styles was even sometimes encased in brick.

139 Brick chimneys on terrace housing for mineworkers; Easington, Co. Durham; late 19C.

140 Castellated stone stack on Gothick country house; Stout's Hill, Uley, Gloucestershire; 1743.

141 Vernacular round stone stacks with slate tops on cottage; Grasmere, Cumbria.

142 Arts and Crafts brick stacks on model housing; Port Sunlight, Cheshire; c. 1900.

143 Rendered stack; Haddenham, Buckinghamshire; 1960s.

144 Coloured metal flue in chimney position on terrace; Greenwich Millennium Village, London; 2000.

Cladding

Tile-hanging (also known as weather-tiling), slate-hanging and weatherboarding or clapboard were all originally used to protect timber-framed, brick or stone walls from the extremes of the British climate. Frequently, the upper storey only was clad with the overlapping tiles, slates or boards which tilted out at the base to deflect water away from the wall. These solutions were regional and the earliest examples probably date from the 17th century. Tile-hanging and weatherboarding are both particularly characteristic of, although not exclusive to, south-east England whereas slate-hanging is mainly found in Devon and Cornwall.

Tiles designed to imitate brick, known as mathematical tiles, were an invention of the Georgian period and used to clad houses. Initially this was probably a way of updating an earlier house by disguising a timber-frame or altered window patterns. After the onset of the 1784 brick tax, they were also used on new buildings.

In many cases cladding was added as an improvement and tended to date from the later Georgian period. It was also, however, an opportunity for gentle ornamentation, as decoratively shaped tiles created interesting effects of light and shade and contrasting coloured slate and clay tiles further enriched the patterning. J. C. Loudon wrote in his *Encyclopedia of Cottage, Farm and Villa Architecture* (1833) that tile-hanging gave a 'homely and comfortable appearance'. Tile-hanging made the transition to the ordinary early 20th-century house with its token section applied to gable or bay, but once the tiles were machine-made they lost their wobbly charm. Weatherboarding fared better and 'waney-edged' (edges untrimmed) elm boards were a popular feature in the early part of the century.

Architecture of the 1950s and 1960s made much use of contrasting sections of cladding, as prefabricated panels and new materials such as plastics increased the options of colour and texture. Cladding with thin metal sheeting was a late 20th-century direction.

145 Black mathematical tiles applied onto brick terrace; Brighton, Sussex; terrace 1798–1807, tiles applied later.

146 Tile hanging and weatherboarding on estate cottages; Groombridge, Kent.

| 145 | | 147 | 148 | 149 | 150 |
| 146 | | 151 | 152 | 153 | 154 |

147 Decorative slate-hanging in two colours, living accommodation above shop; Dartmouth, Devon; c. 1880.

148 Cladding with cement tiles, Span housing development; Blackheath, London; 1950s.

149 Tile hanging decoration above window; Reading, Berkshire; c. 1870.

150 Pre-cast concrete 'weatherboard' on public housing; Writtle, Essex; 1950s.

151 Weatherboarded cottage; Roxwell, Essex.

152 Tile-hung upper storey on cottage; Petworth, Sussex.

153 Slate-hung house; St Ives, Cornwall; 18C.

154 Timber cladding on upper storey of rebuilt mews; Highbury, London; 1990s.

Coade Stone

Coade stone was manufactured in Lambeth from 1769 until 1821. During its most successful period the company was run by Eleanor Coade and after her death by a relation, William Croggan, who then sold the business on. The moulds and models were finally bought by a sculptor, J. M. Blashfield, who had worked with the firm and who moved it to Stamford in Lincolnshire.

This patent stone provided a very extensive range of external embellishments: keystones, plaques, paterae, friezes, capitals, bas-reliefs, rusticated blocks, voussoirs, caryatids, statues, vases, urns, even garden seats (as well as non-domestic ornamentation such as figures of Britannia or Royal Coats of Arms) The great success of Coade stone stemmed from its ability to provide fashionable ornament in quantity. This was extremely useful for the builders and architects of the fast-expanding terraces and squares of London and other cities, particularly as the Building Act of 1774 put further restrictions on the use of wood on façades as a fire-prevention measure.

Coade stone was especially suitable for the delicate exterior detail applied on façades and popularised by Robert Adam during the last quarter of the 18th century. The company responded quickly to changing fashions, and produced pieces in Neo-Classical, Greek Revival and Egyptian styles. Among the most popular and typical of their details were the rusticated blocks used as quoins and keystones, and the voussoirs which emphasised the arched openings for windows and doors. These were termed vermiculated (random groovings, like a worm-cast) congelated (like icicles) or punctured (with dots and spots). Equally popular were keystones ornamented with female masks, classical gods and satyr heads, bucrania and ram's heads, which gave individuality to otherwise uniform doorways on terraces and squares. Coade was the earliest company to produce an artificial stone, but in the 19th century many followed on in the mass-production of exterior ornamentation.

155 Mask keystone with vermiculated voussoirs over doorcase; Marylebone, London; late 1770s.

156 Ram's head and festoon on frieze, palmettes and egg and dart on capital of porch; Chandos House, Marylebone, London; c. 1770.

157 Fluted fan over doorcase; Bloomsbury; London; c. 1780–90.

158 Panel of guilloche pattern; Adam Street, London; c. 1770.

159 Bacchic mask keystone over doorcase; Marylebone, London; c. 1790.

160 Male herm supporting porch; Schomberg House, London; 1791.

161 Female herms on terrace; Regent's Park, London; 1820–21.

162 Panel with festoon, ribbons and paterae; Home House, Portman Square, London; 1775.

Conversions

Conversions have often been the catalyst for original and imaginative designs for living. Principally a 20th-century exercise in recycling redundant buildings, which are often of architectural interest and importance, conversions are particularly popular at times when materials and labour are hard to come by, or where building land is scarce.

Conversions

The conversion of other structures into houses is driven by a combination of factors: redundancy of building type, shortage of housing and desirability of the site. One of the earliest examples is the stone-built monastic farm buildings intended to shelter sheep at Bibury in Gloucestershire which, during the 17th century, were converted into a row of cottages. Another unusually early conversion exists at Paignton in Devon, where in 1853 a newly redundant Martello tower turned into an Indian-style seaside house.

The rush for conversion started after World War II. Over three million houses had been damaged by enemy action and building materials were in short supply, so canal barges, railway carriages and even buses were rapidly converted into temporary homes. Permanent solutions were found by the conversion of small redundant buildings such as mews (originally intended for horses, carriages and grooms) behind the terraces and squares in the grander parts of town. These were relatively simple to convert into fashionably compact houses, as were coach houses and stables attached to village and town houses. In the countryside redundant windmills and oast houses were popular choices in the 1950s and 1960s as well as workshops of declining rural trades such as forges and sail lofts. However the most common conversion during the last three decades of the 20th century was the barn and the farmyard. Farming during the post-war period became increasingly specialised and the mixed farm with its yard consisting of milking parlours, pigsties, sheep pens and assorted barns and granaries was disappearing, leaving a variety of buildings empty. In desirable rural locations, where permission to build new houses was hard to get, such conversions also met the increasing demand for holiday homes. Experiments were even made with relatively recent building types such as the metal grain silo, converted into an adjunct to a house.

163 Redundant technology: a windmill that worked as a wind-powered drainage pump on low-lying land. It was converted into a holiday cottage during the 1960s with the removal of all the machinery and the addition of a glazed structure wrapping around the tower. Reedham Ferry, Norfolk.

164 'Container City' studios and live/work spaces designed by Nicholas Lacey & Partners and constructed from converted steel shipping containers. They were erected on derelict dockland in 2002 using 80 per cent recycled building material. Trinity Buoy Wharf, East London.

From the 1970s onwards small village schools with declining rolls were perceived as educationally unsuitable and uneconomic; many closed and these too became further grist to the conversion mill. The same fate awaited many non-denominational chapels and churches. The Pastoral Measure of 1968 noted that the Church of England considered the upkeep of small rural churches an intolerable drain on resources, and that those that were not of great historical interest could be appropriately converted into domestic housing. The first was completed in 1972. Non-denominational chapels, often not listed as of architectural importance, were converted in greater numbers during the same period. Dr Beeching's 1963 plan for the closure of six thousand miles of unprofitable railway lines left in its wake several thousand unwanted railway stations, all ripe for conversion.

165 In the 1920s railway carriages were cheaply acquired and easily moved and they could provide an economic home or holiday cottage which could be extended over time. Their temporary nature made them easy to establish on marginal land. Selsey, Sussex.

166 Barn conversion, featuring black-painted weatherboarding, the original finish would have been a weatherproof coat of black bitumen typical of farm buildings, particularly in East Anglia. Saffron Walden, Essex.

167 Martello tower built in the early 19C, first converted in 1853 into a whimsical seaside house with a combination of Indian and castle-style ornament. Paignton, Devon.

168 A straightforward conversion from pub to private house requiring little alteration but retaining the fine ironwork sign. Due to drink-driving laws and the cheap price of supermarket alcohol over 6,000 pubs closed between 2005 and 2010. Stebbing, Essex.

169 Schisms and new sects prompted the building of a considerable number of Non-conformist chapels, particularly in the 19C. This Wesleyan Methodist Chapel built in 1838 and restored in 1893 was converted into two apartments in 2008. Holt, Norfolk.

170 Selwood Printing Works, a Victorian stone factory built to impress in 1866 with arcaded brick Romanesque Revival-style window openings and carved datestones. By the 1980s it was empty and derelict, but finally was converted into 12 flats and 10 houses in 2000, a contributing factor in the town's regeneration. Frome, Somerset.

171 Feed mill dating from the 1940s converted in 2001 into two flats with studios; steel panels with black finish replaced the original corrugated asbestos cladding. Bruton, Somerset.

165		
166	168	
		169 170
167	171	

The gradual acceptance by the British of the desirability, or necessity, of living in a flat made viable the conversion of large urban buildings — mills and factories — which were in plentiful supply following the post-war decline of Britain's manufacturing base. Modern container ports ousted the old city ports such as London, Cardiff, Gloucester and Liverpool, leaving them with vast empty docklands full of empty buildings and warehouses. Many have been converted into flats, often combined with studio or work space, on the American loft model. Continued pressure on housing means that there is little that the British cannot convert into housing — lunatic asylums, electricity sub-stations, water towers, seaman's missions, even office blocks — the latter reversing a trend of the first part of the 20th century when houses were more likely to be converted into offices.

Corrugated Iron

The invention in the late 1820s of corrugated iron is credited to the founder of the Institute of Engineers, Henry Robinson Palmer. It was immediately recognised as invaluable for building large roof spans, and therefore particularly useful in the construction of barns and warehouses. One of the first people to write about it was J. C. Loudon in his *Encyclopaedia of Cottage, Farm and Villa Architecture* (1833), recommending its use in door panels, cottage roofs and 'portable houses'. Loudon pointed out that its durability depended on the application of oil or tar paints, and that iron cottages should be covered in evergreen creeper 'to moderate the effect of changes in the exterior temperature'.

Corrugated iron was light and easily transported by rail (or by ship to distant colonies), and manufacturers such as Boulton and Paul of Norwich and William Cooper of the Old Kent Road in London responded by producing large ranges of 'portable' or prefabricated houses, cottages and bungalows as well as cricket pavilions, churches, billiard rooms, village halls and mission rooms. The relative cheapness of corrugated iron buildings (only a brick foundation was required) meant that they were popular for holiday and seaside homes, fishing and hunting lodges. They also provided low-cost housing for gardeners, gamekeepers and estate workers, which was useful in remote places where the transport of traditional building materials was problematic.

Cooper's turn-of-the-century catalogue describes the material used in its houses as being 'standard Birmingham gauge only, truly and evenly corrugated, thickly coated with pure Silesian spelter'. Cooper's also supplied ornamental iron pinnacles and roof cresting in 'approved Gothic designs'. However, in many areas, restrictive by-laws prevented the proliferation of such buildings.

172 Iron porch with corrugated iron roof on terrace; Beccles, Suffolk; late 19C.

173 House with double-storey wooden balcony; Medstead, Hampshire; late 19C/early 20C.

172		174	175	
173			177	178
		176	179	180

174 Corrugated iron porch roof and cottage roof; Mudford, Somerset.

175 Bungalow with wooden bargeboards and iron roof cresting; Amberley, Gloucestershire; early 20C.

176 Corrugated iron roof, public housing; Queen Camel, Somerset; 1925.

177 Bungalow with brick chimneys and bay window; Boughton, Kent; late 19C/early 20C.

178 Holiday cottage with wooden balcony; Aberdaron, Gwynedd; early 20C.

179 Corrugated iron replacing stone or thatch as roof; Dinton, Wiltshire.

180 Corrugated iron porch with slate roof; Plockton, Highlands.

Cottages

The cottage has long been associated with rural idyll. Built from local materials it represents vernacular architecture, and carries with it the idea of a simple life. Its uses range from a home for agricultural workers — not necessarily idyllic — to a permanent or part-time retreat for stressed city-dwellers.

Cottages

Traditionally cottages were considered primitive dwellings for people working on the land. Chaucer, in *The Nun's Priest's Tale*, describes the late 14th-century cottage of a poor old widow who, with her two daughters, occupies two sooty rooms, surrounded by a yard and lives off her chickens, three pigs, three cows and a sheep. Many cottages probably lasted for only a couple of generations, but others survived and were adapted over the centuries. Dating a cottage is difficult precisely because of the layers of its accretions and improvements: extra chimneys, a layer of plaster for weatherproofing, extensions, enlarged windows, upper storeys or decorative features such as bargeboards and porches. Valuable building material was frequently re-used: a sturdy oak beam originally hewn in the Middle Ages or a good block of stone might have been appropriated from an abandoned castle or monastery nearby.

The aspect and history of a cottage is inextricably intertwined with the geographical, social and economic factors of the area in which it was built. The insecurities inherent in the medieval feudal system meant that the average serf was more likely to live in a hovel rather than something permanent. This situation changed during the Tudor period as people increasingly leased land, becoming smallholders. Village settlements varied. Some cottages had naturally grown up around castles, churches and religious foundations, others in so-called 'closed' villages clustered round one landowner on whom their well-being depended; others were sprawling 'open' villages with the land owned independently. The existence of large tracts of common land tempted many to encroach on it and appropriate a plot for their cottage, or to squat along the road, taking a long sliver of land for their own. In the late 16th century, as building increased, so specific skills developed: masons, thatchers, tilers, carpenters emerged and alongside them the 'cottage industries' — the wool workers, tanners and weavers.

181 One-up one-down cottage built in materials traditional in North Norfolk, flint walls with brick. Flints are found in chalk, and where a chalk cliff meets the sea, smooth flints are easily picked off the beach. The pantile roof is also characteristic of the area. Historically they were laid over a sub-roof of reeds and hair mortar. Burnham Market, Norfolk.

182 Cottage c. 1895, built by landowner for his tenant in decorative vernacular style with a tile-hung upper storey with alternating rectangular and pointed tiles, a pattern echoed by the roof tiles. The irregular rubblestone is emphasised at ground level. Stedham, Sussex.

Cottages

In the 18th century the lives of cottagers changed. As land became more profitable, the concept of private land was extended. Landowners enclosed village fields and commons, where traditionally cottagers had enjoyed rights to graze animals and gather firewood. Many old cottages were swept away during this process causing considerable hardship. Increasingly wealthy landowners established themselves in large country houses which were fashionably set in landscaped parkland. For reasons both philanthropic and aesthetic, clusters of existing unsightly hovels were frequently removed from the house's sightlines and replaced with consciously picturesque, and improved, living quarters for cottagers. Extreme versions, termed *cottages ornés*, were often polygonal, decorated with tall patterned chimneys, overhanging eaves, elaborate thatching, fancy glazing on the windows and loggias with seats.

Simultaneously, the idea of the cottage as a place in which the genteel classes could enjoy tranquil country life emerged. Fanny Burney wrote in her journal in 1773: 'Mr & Mrs Rishton are turned into absolute hermits for this summer, they have left Bath, and are to Tingmouth [sic] in Devonshire where they have taken a *cottage* rather than a house'. The cottage as a retreat for holidays and weekends grew in popularity over the subsequent two centuries, as holiday-makers' horizons were expanded first through railways, then motorways. Sporadic depressions in farming during the late 19th and early 20th centuries was followed by the mechanisation of farm work, and the consequent reduction of agricultural jobs resulted in many farm cottages being sold off. These tended to be dwellings that might be most attractive to the general buyer — older and prettier, but in need of restoration, improvement and investment. This led to a concern about suitable housing for genuine agricultural workers and their families which landowners could afford to build, and workers afford to rent. The Cheap Cottage Exhibition at Letchworth in 1905 was one of several initiatives to devise economic rural housing. The insistence of many authorities that traditional materials must be used had increased building costs beyond the means of some farmers and landowners.

183 Rose Cottage, one of a group of nine picturesque cottages built in 1810 and designed by John Nash for landowner John Harford to house his elderly retainers. Characteristic of the style are the asymmetric form, diamond lattice casement windows, diagonally set triple chimney, gables, porch and outside bench. Blaise Hamlet, Bristol.

184 Ancient stone cottage with new wheat-straw thatch laid hayrick style. The change from stone to brick on the upper story indicates where the windows would have been altered. Muchelney, Somerset

185 Roadside cottage, with the chimneys clearly added to each gable wall and built high to keep clear of the thatch. The plaster render is washed

'Suffolk pink' a traditional colour in East Anglia. Historically this was made by adding pig's blood to the limewash. Lindsey, Suffolk.

186 Small cottage constructed in 1905 for the Cheap Cottage Exhibition: this was intended to initiate innovative methods and materials in constructing cottages for agricultural workers. They had to be built for under £150, so that they could be let at an affordable £8 p.a.

187 Traditional form of Scottish cottage — low, with dormer windows lighting the upper storey. Rubblestone walls, such as these, have frequently been whitewashed, partly to weatherproof cracks and flaws, but also keeping a cottage sparkling white was a sign of pride. Plockton, Highlands.

188 Side elevation of cottage. The larger proportions of the most recent addition on the front demonstrates the desire for ever higher rooms and larger windows. The tile hanging has acquired a coating of lichen, which only occurs on the rougher surface of hand-made tiles. East Lulworth, Dorset.

189 Thatched and rendered double cottage, the central chimney would have served both ends. East Suffolk.

190 Plain stone cottage built in 1904. Basic four-square design with large stone lintels, sills and canopy over the front door. Dressed stone quoins strengthen the corners of the building which is built from rubblestone (that is pieces that are not evenly hewn or laid in regular courses). Langdale, Cumbria.

Datestones

Datestones appear on all sorts of housing in all periods, ingeniously worked in brick, moulded in plaster, carved in stone and incised in wood. Dates were often combined with the initials of the house-builder or first owner, or two sets of initials marked a wedding and perhaps the beginning of the owners' life in the house. Dates were particularly common on estate cottages, designating the periods during which the landowner improved the lot of his tenant. Equally model housing and dwelling houses were frequently dated. Very early dates are likely to be optimistic suppositions or results of researching by subsequent owners and are not necessarily contemporaneous with the building. New wings and additions were similarly marked. Some years are more 'date conscious' than others, for example Queen Victoria's Golden and Diamond Jubilee years, 1887 and 1897, frequently appear.

191 Painted relief plasterwork; Totnes, Devon; 1585.

192 Painted carved stone door lintel; Askham, Cumbria; 1674.

193 Painted stone label on lintel; Falkland, Fife; 1721.

194 Date and monogram carved on pediment; Clifton Hill House, Bristol; 1747.

195 Keystone; Painswick, Gloucestershire; 1800.

196 Iron plaque on terrace; Elsecar, Yorkshire; 1837.

197 Plaster date plaque on semi-detached villa; St John's Wood, London; 1847.

198 Date over entrance to flats; Chelsea, London; 1886.

199 Stone datestone with carved coronet; Holt, Norfolk; 1887.

200 Stone carved datestone; Wincanton, Somerset; 1891.

201 Terra-cotta panel; Tottenham, London; 1892.

202 Date in mortar on brick; St Osyth, Essex; 1911.

203 Date incised on pebbledash gable on terrace; Acton, London; 1912.

204 Moulded concrete datestone at base of outside gate; Kentish Town, London; 1987.

<table>
<tr><td>191</td><td></td><td>194</td><td>195</td><td></td></tr>
<tr><td>192</td><td></td><td>196</td><td>197</td><td>198</td></tr>
<tr><td>193</td><td></td><td>199</td><td>200</td><td>201</td></tr>
<tr><td></td><td></td><td>202</td><td>203</td><td>204</td></tr>
</table>

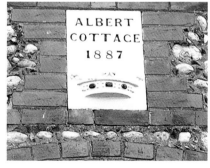

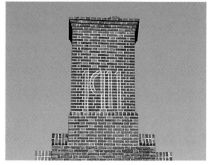

Decorative Plasterwork

Traditionally plaster was made from lime and sand often bulked out with hair, feathers or straw; at a later date cement was added. It was used on timber-frame buildings (sometimes covering up all timber work) and also on stone.

Although associated with interior decoration, plaster has frequently been used for the decoration of exteriors. Pargetting describes the technique of making patterns on the plaster itself and is particularly characteristic of East Anglian houses. Early examples date from the 17th century, but the designs have usually been re-worked and augmented. At their simplest they are geometric repeat patterns incised on the wet plaster with combs, sticks, stamps or even wickerwork, creating a far more interesting surface than plain plaster. More elaborate patterns were reliefs which were either moulded or worked freehand, the body of the relief design created by animal hair mixed in with the plaster.

In some cases plasterwork was used to decorate the building with fashionable motifs and to cover up and update timber-framing, in competition with stone carving or cut brick. Typically 17th-century ornamentation might include swags of fruit and flowers, columns or masks.

Decorative plasterwork was revived in the late 19th century, the white plaster creating a strong contrast to red brick. The patterns filled in gables and ran along cornices and, as in earlier examples, were a way of displaying up-to-date decoration such as Art Nouveau swirls and plant forms. Sgraffito is a technique more traditionally used in Northern and Eastern Europe, but which occasionally appears on British buildings. Two contrasting layers of plaster are laid one on top of the other, and the top layer is then scraped off, creating a two-coloured design. Pargetting was revived in the 20th century but often on cement-based plaster which produced a hard-edged, more mechanical result.

205 Plaster volutes, rustication and keystone masks; Totnes, Devon; late 17C.

206 Pargetted gable; Saffron Walden, Essex; 17C on 15C house.

207 Pargetted date in cartouche on porch; Chelsworth, Suffolk; 1689.

208 Incised decoration on oriel window; Scotney Castle, Kent; 19C restoration.

209 Pargetted diaper patterns; Saffron Walden, Essex; 17C/18C.

210 Modern plasterwork decoration in pargetted style on cottage; Writtle, Essex.

211 Plaster relief on cornice, ribbons and festoons; Hampstead, London; c. 1880.

212 Pargetting on upper storey; Clare, Suffolk; 17C plaster on 15C house.

213 Sgraffito decoration on bungalow; Birchington-on-Sea, Kent; 1882.

214 Relief plasterwork between ground- and first-floor windows; St John's Wood, London; 1890s.

		207	208	209
205		210	211	213	214
206		212			

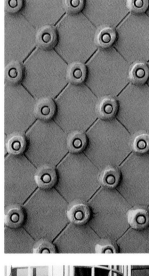

Doors

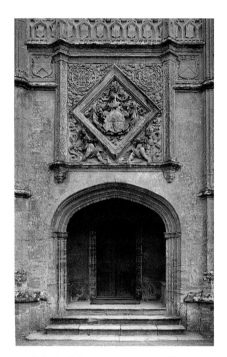

215 Principal doorway surmounted by heraldic escutcheon; Montacute House, Somerset; 1590s.

216 Pair of carved wooden hooded canopies; City of London; 1703.

217 Carved, initialled and dated lintel stone; Grewelthorpe, Yorkshire; 1706.

218 Carved stone motto on courtier's house with date and builder's marks ('Contentment is Great Riches'); Falkland, Fife; 1607.

The principal entrance of a house is the cynosure, and thus where, if there is to be ornamental detail, it can make maximum impact. It is also the part of the house most susceptible to alteration, either for practical reasons of deterioration or to keep up with changing fashion.

Relatively few medieval houses were grand enough to have a decorated front entrance, and those that did followed the prevailing arch forms in succession: the round-headed Anglo-Norman, pointed Gothic, then the shallow segmental version popular in the late 15th century. Early doors were probably no more than vertical planks, strengthened horizontally at the back and hung on iron strap hinges. Nail patterns on the boarding or ornamental shaping of the ironwork expressed individuality. Rarely, the wood might be decorated, like contemporary furniture, with linen-fold panelling or Gothic arcading, but serviceability and security would have been the principal aim. Such basic planked doors remained the norm for cottage and back doors.

From the 16th century the square lintel was most usual — the spot for datestones, builder's initials, mason's marks or carving. The Tudors and Stuarts, particularly the *nouveaux riches*, were also enthusiastic about displays of heraldry, and the front entrance was clearly the obvious place for it. The Jacobeans applied their love of elaborate panelling and mouldings to the design of their front doors, but by the late 17th and early 18th centuries the panels had been simplified and usually reduced to six or eight per door.

The vocabulary of Classicism was the impetus for a complete change in door style from around the 1680s. Three basic shapes emerged: a straight projecting cornice supported on two carved console brackets; the coved arched hood, typically carved with a shell motif; and the doorcase with a Classical pediment (which varied in shape: segmental, broken, swan neck or the plain triangular which superseded the other types by the mid 18th century). In all cases the sides were flanked with columns or pilasters: these were usually Ionic

or Doric which were considered suitably robust for an exterior. Fluted columns or pilasters and a decorated frieze further enriched the look of the doorcase, as did the occasional appearances of rarities such as the spiral column.

Builders and craftsmen, even in remote parts of the country, could refer to pattern books to incorporate fashionable variations. James Gibbs's *Book of Architecture containing Designs of Buildings and Ornaments* (1728) introduced the distinctive exaggerated blocking around doorcases which was used well past the middle of the century and was copied in later, cheaper pattern books. The lifespan of books such as Gibbs's and his imitators was long, which meant that builders were often still referring to their designs long after they were in the vanguard of fashion. Isaac Ware in his *Complete Body of Architecture* (1756) gave a clear idea of the importance of the design of the principal door and the need to build it correctly: '(We) shall recommend the care of it to the architect's most serious thought. If any error is committed, it is obvious to the first eye that is cast upon the building; and it is an unlucky one, for this reason, that will put the vulgar in mind of the builder's stumbling at the threshold of his undertaking'.

The raised reception floor above a ground or semi-basement service floor was a further form copied from Renaissance architecture, where the *piano nobile* was always on the first floor. This necessitated a flight of steps leading up to the main entrance which could be embellished with balustrading or sculpture to emphasize its importance. Such steps up to the front door, even if reduced to two or three, remained a marker for a house of substance up to the end of the 19th century, and made a clear separation from the servants' or tradesmen's entrances. On working-class terrace houses where front doors opened straight onto the street a clean, white front step was a mark of respectability and good housekeeping.

From the late Georgian period the arched door opening was prevalent and the semi-circle above the door became a fanlight which allowed light into the hallway. Ornamental wood and stone doorframes were rapidly disappearing by the 1770s: rather, the entrance was marked with stucco and Coade stone ornaments — keystones, quoins and rusticated blocks. The delicate patterns of the fanlight became the focus of the front door.

219 Six-panelled door with lights (probably inserted later); Chilcombe, Dorset; second half of 18C.

Regency doors eschewed panelling in favour of strongly vertical designs with incised decoration and reeding, and sometimes circular bull's-eye panels. Porches and porticos fitted the style and framed the door, often made with increasingly available cast iron. The fashionable balconies and verandas shielded the house from light and, to compensate, glazed doors or French windows were introduced.

The eclecticism of Victorian architecture led to a range of far more complicated doors, with a concentration of detail and ornament. Increasingly houses had names or numbers which had to be displayed, and door knockers, bells and letterboxes became essential. With the asymmetry of Victorian style the porch and gable were prominent so the front door itself sometimes almost disappeared from view. Ornament had become relatively cheap so a front entrance could easily look impressive with a polychrome gabled porch, granite pillars, stained-glass door lights, encaustic tile steps and path and sets of brass door furniture. There was usually some variation on the column either side of the door, which might sprout composite stone Gothic foliage, or even some Egyptian motif. A much-loved feature of Victorian life and ornament was the motto, and it was in this period that a carved stone motto such as 'God's Providence is Mine Inheritance' or more sportively on a country house 'Fay ce Voudras' [Do as you will] would face the visitor as he approached the front door. For flats the entrance doors were particularly important, since it was by the quantity and quality of ornamentation that the grandeur of the mansion block could be assessed. By contrast the blocks of working-class lodgings, that might at a glance be of similar scale and shape, had open access up a staircase with individual doors leading off walkways at every level, and often visible from the street.

While a large proportion of the population still had servants, it was considered necessary in most houses to have a separate entrance which led straight into the kitchen for servants and for tradesmen's deliveries. This would either be the back door or the door in the basement area which was always utilitarian in design, and often involved a separate path or gate. When both servants and deliveries went into decline after World War II more thought was given to the design of the back door and utilities.

The Queen Anne Revival style of the 1880s brought back the emphasis on framing the door: big, deep doorcases with elaborate pediments or Dutch gables and terra-cotta ornamention, typically datestones, swags of fruit and pots of sunflowers and lilies. Unlike the uniform doors on terrace houses this type of house, usually detached and substantial, had a door that fought to be distinctive through a range of panelling, carving and glazing picked out from the numerous building-trade catalogues.

In the design of Arts and Crafts-inspired houses the front door was often recessed back from the façade within an arched nook, a form that remained a standard feature on suburban housing well into the interwar period. Doors themselves were again of simple planking or tongue-and-groove. Door furniture had the look of hand-wrought iron rather than shiny brass. During this period most doors had some glazed panels: light came in but privacy was retained with coloured glass or etched frosted glass. These effects stayed in favour well into the 1930s, expressing stylishness and individuality through their design: Gothic quatrefoils and fleurs-de-lys, naturalistic birds and flowers, Art Nouveau plant forms, Edwardian wreaths, Art Deco chevrons or a mock Tudor galleon in full sail. Such ornamentation also clearly set private houses apart from public housing.

By the 1930s people wanted and expected lighter houses and the amount of door glazing increased. The production of toughened plate glass meant that it was possible to produce a metal and glass door which set no limitations on design and which was sufficiently sturdy for an exterior. By the 1950s panelling looked outdated, and most designs were for flush doors with strips of glazing flanking the door like columns, or confined to a neat geometric square or circle within it. In the security-conscious 21st century there has been a move towards a more fortified look, achieved with steel rather than relatively fragile wood.

220 Doors on terrace housing for workers at Courtauld's; Halstead, Essex; c. 1900.

221 Plate glass and ironwork door; Highgate, London; late 1950s/1960s.

Vernacular and Early Doors

222 Stone fragments of Norman church door frame on 19C cottage; Sherborne, Gloucestershire.

223 Linenfold panelling on courtyard doors; Paycocke's, Coggeshall, Essex; c.1500.

224 Cottage door with horseshoe nailed on wooden lintel; Asthall, Oxfordshire.

225 Boarded door with filleted joints on manor house; Great Chalfield, Wiltshire; late 15C/early 16C.

226 Wooden lintel and planked door; Arlington Row, Bibury, Oxfordshire; 14C barns converted to cottages in 17C.

227 Panelled door; Burton Constable Hall, East Riding, Yorkshire; 1601.

228 Tongue-and-groove boarded door under stone canopy; Taynton, Oxfordshire.

229 Planked door with repair scarfed in at base and strap hinges; Burford, Oxfordshire; stone arched opening 15C/16C.

230 Wide planked door with base repairs; Sutton Courtenay, Oxfordshire; 17C.

231 Cottage door with stone lintel, jambs and steps; Slaidburn, Lancashire.

232 Doorcase with shell hood, pargetted ornament above; Newport, Essex; 1692.

233 Tongue-and-groove boarded door, estate cottage with ceramic number; Blickling, Norfolk.

222	223	224	225	226	227	228	229
				230	231	232	233

18th-Century Doors

234 Carved wooden canopy door; Westminster, London; 1704.

235 Carved stone doorcase with broken pediment canopy and segmental-headed door; Uley, Gloucestershire; early 18C.

236 Painted carved shell-headed doorcase, 6-panelled door; Bampton, Oxfordshire; early 18C.

237 Stone segmental pediment doorcase with columns, 12-panelled door; Lancaster; 1720s.

238 Wood segmental pediment doorcase with spiral columns, 10-panelled door; King's Lynn, Norfolk; early 18C.

239 Six-panelled door with sidelights and fanlight, set within rusticated arch; Charlotte Square, New Town, Edinburgh; 1791.

240 Pedimented doorcase with rusticated or Gibbs surround, 4-panelled door; Bury St Edmunds, Suffolk; mid-18C.

241 Arched doorway with fanlight on terrace; Islington, London; 1786.

242 Canopy doorcase on terrace; Westminster, London; late 1720s.

243 Doorcase with fluted columns and pediment; Hatfield, Hertfordshire; mid-18C.

234	234	235	238	239	240	241
	236	237	242	243		

19th-Century Doors

244 245 246 247 248 249 250 251	252 253 254 255

244 Arched doorcase with fanlight on terrace; Clapton, London; c. 1820.

245 Stucco doorway in Egyptian style with obelisks and sphinxes; Islington, London; c. 1830.

246 Gothic Revival stucco doorway, with pierced quatrefoil lights; Islington, London; 1838–45.

247 Stone doorcase with incised decoration; Morningside, Edinburgh; c. 1870.

248 Gothic Revival stone porch; Hackney, London; mid 19C.

249 Brick terrace door with stone lintel and keystone; Southwold, Suffolk; c. 1860–70.

250 Boarded door with decorative Gothic Revival ironwork; North Oxford; 1870s.

251 Arched doorway encompassing door and hall oriel window; Hampstead, London; late 19C/early 20C.

252 Glasgow School doorcase with mosaic decoration on artist Jessie M. King's house; Kirkcudbright, Dumfries and Galloway; c. 1890.

253 Entrance to mansion block; Maida Vale, London; c.1890–1900.

254 Brick and pebbledash terrace; Port Sunlight, Cheshire; late 19C/early 20C.

255 Door with stained glass panel, granite-pillared porch; Fulham, London; late 19C/early 20C.

20th-Century Doors

256 Entrance to small block of flats, dated keystone; Chelsea, London; 1911.

257 Rendered brick door surround; Gidea Park, Essex; 1934.

258 Entrance to block of flats in stone and brick; Highgate, London; 1934.

259 Suburban semi-detached door, galleon under full sail in stained-glass panel; Colchester, Essex; 1920s.

260 Arched door and sidelights; Highgate, London; late 1920s.

261 Concrete canopy and glass sidelights on public housing; Islington, London; 1950s.

262 Terrace housing; Bankside, London; 1980s.

263 Flush door on entrance to small block of flats; Bloomsbury, London; early 1990s.

264 Art Deco ironwork against glass door; Hendon, London; 1930s.

265 Entrance to small block of flats; Limehouse, London; c. 2000.

266 Front door and wall in glass; Hampstead, London; 1975.

267 Security door on terrace house refurbished into flats; Camden, London; late 1990s.

Door Furniture

Until the end of the 18th century door furniture (knobs, handles, knockers or locks) would have been made of iron or wood or, if extremely grand, bronze. Doors were either barred and bolted from the inside or fitted with box- or rim-locks fixed to the inside of the door, which opened with large unwieldy keys; however these were extremely easy to pick. Two inventors solved this problem: Joseph Bramah patented a mortise lock in 1784, followed by Jeremiah Chubb in 1818, both producing improved and more impenetrable locks using smaller keys. Later in the century the American Linus Yale patented various locks with small, flat keys which he manufactured from 1868 onwards.

As horse-drawn traffic of the 18th century created muddy and dirty roads, Robert Adam included a cast-iron boot scraper (incorporating his favourite anthemion motif) on one of the houses of his Adelphi development in around 1770. Boot scrapers became a fairly standard feature, often inserted into the wall beside the front door or fixed into the doorstep. In towns and cities before street lighting, iron snuffers were fixed beside the door for link boys to extinguish their torches on arrival.

Brass knockers started appearing in the late 18th century as casting techniques improved. Fashionable motifs included gryphons, female masks, lion's heads or sphinxes. Characteristic Victorian motifs include the woman's hand and the fox mask. Bells tended to supplant knockers from the 1830s onwards when brass or iron bell pushes or pulls appeared beside front door.

Although the Penny Post was introduced in 1840, the need for letter-boxes was not felt for about forty years by which time the volume of post had grown enormously — augmented by the introduction of the Christmas card, postcard and Valentine — and the postman no longer had time to knock on each door to deliver the mail.

268 Wrought ironwork knocker and strap hinge; Coggeshall, Essex.

269 Cast iron bootscraper in anthemion and paw-foot motifs; Westminster, London; 1770s.

268	270 271 272 273	
269	274 275 276 277	

270 Brass keyhole and door handle; Salisbury, Wiltshire; early 19C.

271 Brass knocker of female mask; Bath; early 19C pattern.

272 Lyre knocker; Warwick, Warwickshire; 19C.

273 Brass vertical letterbox; Hadleigh, Suffolk; late 19C/early 20C.

274 Cast iron fox mask doorknocker on cottage; Holkham, Norfolk; late 19C/early 20C.

275 Brass bells for 'Servants' and 'Visitors' fixed on gateposts; Kensington, London; late 19C.

276 Cast-iron handle-cum-knocker; Alyth, Perthshire; 19C.

277 Snuffer for extinguishing link boys' torches; Bath; late 18C/early 19C.

Fanlights

The arched opening, whether for doors or windows, was one of the most easily assimilated elements of Classicism, and a radiating pattern was the most obvious way of decorating the space. The fanlight, set under a triangular, pedimented doorcase, became one of the most ubiquitous features of the mid-18th century, and cabinet-makers created inventive rococo patterns for the glazing bars. Early examples from the 1720s looked chunky as the radiating pattern was either fretted out of solid timber, carved, or produced by placing an ironwork grill in front of the glass. Some designs were published, for example in John Crunden's pattern book *Modern or Ornamental Door Tops* (1770) which illustrated both fan-shaped and rectangular windows. An early instance of home improvement, fanlights were often inserted into earlier doors.

The fanlight is closely associated with the style of the Adam Brothers who translated the Venetian or Palladian window most precisely into the door form by emphasising the arch over the door and taking away any pediments. In addition they included lintel-to-floor side-lights, which allowed the fanlight to be far larger, and become the principal ornamental feature of the doorway. Much greater delicacy of fanlight ornament was achieved by the use of very slim glazing bars as well as cast lead, brass or composition motifs soldered onto the exterior of the glass. Ingenious alternative patterns were placed above doors on flat-fronted terrace housing well into the 19th century. Regency fanlights were often composed of concentric circles and loops, and increasingly the lights were rectangular.

Today, the easy availability of 'off-the-shelf Georgian' dropped fanlight doors has meant the loss of thousands of original and more interesting features.

278 Gothick doorcase with matching fanlight tracery and panelling; Gloucester; late 18C.

279 Fanlight under pediment, wooden glazing bars; Farnham, Surrey; mid-18C.

278		280	281	
279			282	283
		284	285	286

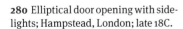

280 Elliptical door opening with side-lights; Hampstead, London; late 18C.

281 Pedimented doorcase with fanlight incorporating lantern fitting; Clifton, Bristol; 18C doorcase, early 19C fanlight.

282 Arched doorcase with metal glazing bars; Salisbury, Wiltshire; late 18C.

283 Canopy doorcase with wooden fanlight; Holborn, London; 1730s.

284 Arched doorcase with fanlight and side-lights; Bloomsbury, London; 1776–86.

285 Arched door opening with fanlight; Islington, London; c. 1840.

286 Rectangular fanlight with metal glazing bars; Hammersmith, London; late 18C.

Farmhouses

The defining characteristic of a farmhouse was traditionally its function — the central hub of the farms that were crucial contributors to the well-being of the nation. They have been adapted and extended in many ways to meet changing patterns of agricultural and country life.

Farmhouses

287

288

289

A farmhouse reflects the state of the rural economy: it is improved and expanded in good times and left simply to survive in bad. The layout of the house in relation to its farm buildings often reflects contemporary agricultural practice. It is most likely to be vernacular in style: purpose and need generally dominate the design and materials are sourced from the immediate vicinity whether timber-frame, stone or brick, or roofed in stone, slate, tile or thatch. The siting of a farmhouse is determined by the lie of the land, prevailing climate and access to water as well as the type of farming practised. Alongside the house there are farm buildings, the most striking of which is usually the barn.

The most primitive form of agricultural property was the medieval longhouse, which provided relatively warm and dry accommodation for the owner, his family and his animals. A common entrance led into a cross-passage that divided the two separate sets of inhabitants. The Tudor period brought the more familiar setting of the farmhouse within its own yard. Tudor yeomen took advantage of the gathering momentum of enclosure to increase their landholdings; trade opportunities were growing and they prospered. In the 16th century the addition of a sturdy chimney to a farmhouse pointed to a man of substance. Although a farmer might want to present a successful image, his house would never be at the forefront of fashion and any exterior ornament or decoration remained simple. On timber-frame properties a plaster render was partly a protection against fire, but it might also be pargetted with panels, foliage and geometric patterns. Stone farmhouses often feature carved datestones and initials to commemorate construction, marriage or the addition of a wing.

During the 18th century landholdings became larger. Land enclosure was accelerated after 1760 as farming became more scientific and profitable, and with this came the appearance of the 'gentleman' farmer, who could make a respectable living from the

287 Small thatched stone farmhouse; this has a 1602 datestone on the chimney stack. Such stones often marked an improvement or addition and it is likely that some of the building is earlier. Stockland, Devon.

288 Stone farmhouse linked to a succession of barns descending in size down the hill, a plan typical of the region. Chastleton, Gloucestershire.

289 Plain mid 19C stone farmhouse in Glen Isla, Perth and Kinross.

Farmhouses

land and take his place in country society. Owners of large estates built large country houses for themselves, but also erected modern farmhouses for their tenant farmers who were working the land to produce the income. For these farmers 'polite' houses were required: this might involve re-fronting the existing vernacular house in the current Georgian style with sash windows and a classical doorframe, or constructing a completely new dwelling. The first pattern book for farmhouses, *Designs and Estimates of Farmhouses etc.,* was published in 1747 by Daniel Garret. The plainness of his designs was only alleviated in two patterns (one with a pedimented doorcase, one with a Diocletian window) and above all he stressed the importance of 'convenience'. The rectangular farmyards included sheds, pigsties, stables, dairies and byres. The Agricultural Revolution had brought changes in farming practices that gradually necessitated larger farmyards and buildings that were required, for example, to house the

290 Early 18C thatched farmhouse, whitewashed brick, with redundant thatched barn in the farmyard converted to house. Happisburgh, Norfolk.

291 Late Georgian farmhouse with adjoining barn and farmyard. The contrasting golden stone ashlar blocks as quoins and window and door surrounds are the only ornamental feature. Halford, Warwickshire.

292 Farmhouse with 17C core, demonstrated by large brick chimney and gable porch. There are later additions and alterations, such as Victorian windows and end lean-to. Fyfield, Essex.

increasing amount of machinery, and to store winter fodder.
The trend of gentrification continued, as William Cobbett noted in his
Rural Rides (1830). Farmhouses, he wrote, had become 'painted shells,
with a mistress within, who is stuck in the place she calls a parlour...the
house too neat for a dirty-shoed carter to be allowed to come into'.
However, over the centuries, the majority of farmhouses have been
built to be plain and serviceable, their intrinsic beauty residing in their
situation and the functional nature of the buildings. It is exactly these
qualities that has made the farmhouse such a desirable house type,
and the adjective 'farmhouse' has come to represent an idyllic way of
country life, associated with warm kitchens and fresh food. During the
20th century the size of a viable farm has increased, and as farms have
amalgamated so farmhouses have been released onto the market.
Now enlarged and glamorised many have become sought-after,
middle-sized family houses, far removed from their agricultural roots.

293 Longhouse pattern of farm, probably
dating from the 17C, which combined
accommodation for farmer and livestock
under the same roof, a typical form in
remote pastoral regions and upland
areas. It was common for the house to
be differentiated from the agricultural
buildings with whitewash. Little
Langdale, Cumbria.

294 An improved and enlarged
farmhouse: the original timber-frame
house, probably dating from the 16C,
has been given a 'polite' Georgian brick
front with pedimented doorcase. The
earlier part has been given Georgian sash
windows. Halstead, Essex.

295 A late 18C or early 19C substantial
farmhouse in local pale red Vale of York
brick with a pantile roof. Malton, Yorkshire.

296 Georgian farmhouse of whitewashed
stone. Local slate has been used for the
canopy porch, window sills and roofing.
Porth Colmon, Gwynedd.

97

Gables and Pediments

Any house with a pitched roof will have a gable at either end, but the gable only becomes a significant feature when it appears on the front elevation. On early timber-frame houses the basic structure was often enlarged by the addition of a cross-wing or end-wings. This was partly in response to the growing practice of having bedrooms on the upper floors, as a gable added both height and light to the attic floor. For the home-owner in the Tudor period more gables meant a more prestigious house, and the addition of a porch often created another gable. Jettied gables looked impressive, towering outwards, sometimes three or four storeys high, but these were forbidden in towns in the 17th century because of the fire risk. Houses in stone, typically manor houses and town houses, followed the same gabled pattern but they tended to be more symmetrical. The space within the triangle was the perfect field for a datestone, heraldic embellishment or sundial.

An alternative to the plain gable emerged around 1570 on the grandest houses, whose owners had access to knowledge of the latest architectural designs from Northern Europe. These Flemish or Dutch gables (brick built like the continental originals) curled and curved, included volutes and small pediments, and were the location for a rich selection of decorative motifs. Sometimes they were stepped ('crow-stepped', 'corbie-stepped'), a version which remained particularly popular in Scotland.

The pediment, supported by columns, is a feature derived from ancient Classical architecture, particularly temple fronts. The architect Palladio adapted it for the façade of villas and thus it was translated onto the fronts of British houses in the mid-17th century.The complete temple front only appears on the grandest houses, but the pediment alone or with pilasters makes frequently appearances on the façades of quite modest houses throughout the 18th century. Unlike a gable the pediment was always placed centrally and bore no relation to the

297	299	
298		300 301

297 Crow-stepped gable, fisherman's cottage; Crail, Fife; 17C/18C.

298 Timber-frame gables; Writtle, Essex; 15C/16C.

299 Classical Revival pediment; Mickley, Yorkshire; 1982.

300 Dutch gable on early 17C brick house; Great Saling Hall, Essex; gable dated 1699.

301 Revived Dutch/Flemish-style gable on brick house; Kensington, London; 1880s.

structure of the house. But like the gable it conveyed grandeur and importance. In addition the pediment was used on terraces to unify the block and to give the impression that the separate houses were one grand whole. Few Neo-Georgian houses of the 20th century have resisted the lure of the pediment, even if only reproduced in miniature over the door.

When the Victorians became bored with Classical symmetry, they quickly revived the gable and expressed it in typically eclectic style as Tudor, Elizabethan or Jacobean. When deep red bricks became fashionable again from the 1870s to 1890s the elaborate Flemish gable was quickly revived. An urban favourite, it was easily attached to high mansion blocks and lofty town houses that filled narrow city plots. With moulded terracotta the options for ornamenting the gable were almost unlimited. For garden cities, garden suburbs and country houses of the early 20th century a tile-hung vernacular style or decorative half-timbering, was deemed more suitable. Partnered with the bay window the gable became the dominant 'value-added' feature of suburban inter-war housing.

A brief vogue for Cape Dutch style from Southern Africa during the early 20th century bought the large curly gable back into fashion, imitating the architecture which the early Dutch settlers had exported from Northern Europe when they colonised Africa in the 17th century.

302 Gable on stone manor house; Trerice, Cornwall; c. 1570.

303 Tudor Revival gables on brick semi-detached villa; Hackney, London; 1839.

304 Cape Dutch-style gable, roughcast and tile; Chelmsford, Essex; c. 1910–20.

305 Jettied gables on timber-frame houses; Bristol; 17C.

306 Pediment on Colston Almshouses; Bristol; 1691.

307 Pediment on terrace; New Town, Edinburgh; c. 1817.

308 Pediment; Winslow Hall, Buckinghamshire; 1700–4.

309 Pediment on gate lodge to Langleys; Great Waltham, Essex; c. 1725

310 Gables on stone and brick double cottage; Manthorpe, Lincolnshire; mid-19C.

311 Stucco pediment on Regency villa; Cheltenham, Gloucestershire; c.1820.

302		305	306	
303		307	308	309
304		310		311

Gates

312 313 314 315   320 321 322 323

316 317 318 319

312 Gate piers with eagles and niches; Mapperton, Dorset; 17C.

313 Gateway into wall surmounted by carved stone fragments on former vicarage; Burford, Oxfordshire; 18C.

314 Stone gateway carved with house name and owners' monogram; Bath; c. 1870s.

315 Aesthetic Movement gates and railings, decorated with sunflowers and japonaiserie fans; Castle Cary, Somerset; 1880s.

316 Yew topiary gate piers in traditional shape; East Bergholt, Suffolk.

317 Cast-iron pedestrian gate at bottom of carriage drive; Coalbrookdale, Shropshire; mid-19C.

318 Cast-iron Gothic Revival gateway with stone gate lodge; Kirkmichael, Ayrshire; mid-19C.

319 Wooden gates in garden wall; Charlton Mackrell, Somerset; early 20C.

320 Boarded garden gate in farm wall; Marlborough, Devon.

321 Home-made gate decorated with ship's half model; Whitby, Yorkshire; early 20C.

322 White picket fence and beech arch; Walthamstow, Essex.

323 Galvanised iron grille gate and fence combined with willow-wattle fencing; Islington, London; 2001.

Glass

Early glass was either blown as a muff-shaped cylinder which was then split lengthwise to produce a sheet or 'brode-glass', or it was spun into discs which came out at roughly four feet in diameter, and was known as crown glass. This method created a central 'bull's-eye' or 'bullion', caused by the removal of the pontil, which was generally discarded or used in less prominent windows. These were purposely produced and used as a decorative feature in the 19th and 20th centuries, either to make the window obscure, or to create a fake Georgian look.

Plate glass was introduced to Britain from France, and made in Lancashire from 1773. Stronger and thicker because it was cast, it was also relatively expensive. Plate glass could also be polished and appear flawless. In the 1880s Chance Brothers introduced sheet glass which was also polished but thinner and cheaper. Combined with the repeal of the glass tax in 1851, expanses of glass could now be used on relatively ordinary houses.

Some of the grandest Tudor houses had sections of coloured and painted glass in their most important windows. Coloured glass, mostly yellow and pale green, was occasionally used in the Regency period along the margins of sash windows and doors.

The Gothic Revival was a catalyst for the reappraisal of stained glass. Coloured glass was thought suitable for prominent places, such as front-door panels, halls and staircase windows. The individual feature of the (often circular) coloured window remained a defining characteristic of suburban houses well into the 1920s.

Glass bricks were originally developed to let light into basement workshops and stores from the street above, but were not used on domestic buildings until the 1930s. They were also a secure way of letting light into halls and stairwells.

Technological developments in the second half of the 20th century expanded the opportunities for using glass in domestic architecture. for example as picture windows, 'curtain' walls, and in ecologically designed housing.

324	327
325	328 329 330 331
326	332

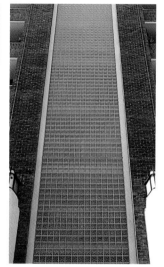

324 Pane of bottle-glass in cottage window; Coggeshall, Essex; 18C/19C.

325 Crown glass window; Widdicombe, Devon; 18C/early 19C.

326 Great Hall window of leaded panes in manor house; Trerice, Cornwall; 1570s.

327 Glass brick façade; Islington, London; 1994.

328 Stained glass front door; Cardiff; c. 1920.

329 Heraldic glass; Haddon Hall, Derbyshire; 16C.

330 Glazed porch with acid-etched decoration and cut red glass; Brighton, Sussex; mid 19C.

331 Glass bricks on stairwell to flats; Camden, London; 1930s.

332 Painted and stained glass; Broadstairs, Kent; c. 1870.

Glazing Patterns

Window glazing bars made up in a rich variety of geometric shapes, and frets were deemed a suitable addition to the Gothick- or Chinoiserie-style buildings that appeared sporadically throughout the second half of the 18th century. The Regency period continued this interest in exotic styles. A rich variety of glazing patterns emerged during the first decades of the 19th century. Arched sash windows on terrace housing showed interesting combinations of curves and circles, details often echoed on the front door or fanlight. Fancy glazing was almost *de rigueur* for the picturesque cottage or *cottage orné*, and could be made up quite cheaply in cast iron in a wide range of lozenges, diamonds and bands that were far more resilient than leaded glazing.

Most ordinary housing of the mid-19th century had newly affordable large panes of glass, but at the end of the century the wheel of fashion turned again and elaborately glazed windows re-emerged. The architect M. Hugh Baillie Scott's instructions were typical: 'The beauty of glass depends entirely on its use in small pieces, in a setting which will make them sparkle and twinkle. The large sheet with its vacant stare, should never be used unless under stress of circumstances'. These windows also signalled expensive ornamentation — the builder's added value — and some were used in conjunction with coloured and painted glass windows and door lights; decorative glazing was often confined to the top one-third of the total window space. In the 20th century lead glazing was used to produce an 'old-worlde' appearance and to suggest craftsmanship. For example, the diamond pane was used in tandem with Mock-Tudor half-timbered ornamentation.

333 Wooden glazing bars on Gothick-style sash window; Stout's Hill, Uley, Gloucestershire; 1743.

334 Leaded glazing on oriel window of cottage orné; Old Warden, Bedfordshire; c. 1840.

333		335 336 337
334		338 339 340 341

335 Wooden glazing bars on sash window; Clifton, Bristol; mid-19C.

336 Wooden glazing bars on Indian- or Oriental-style sash window; Brighton, Sussex; 1830.

337 Cast-iron casement windows; Martock, Somerset; mid-19C.

338 Wooden glazing bars on Gothick-style oriel window; Farnham, Surrey; early 19C.

339 Cast-iron casement windows; Bitton, Gloucestershire; c. 1840.

340 Pointed window on *cottage orné* lodge; Oakhill, Somerset; c. 1790.

341 Cast-iron casement window on lodge; Holkham, Norfolk; c. 1840.

342 Cresting on garden wall; Saffron Walden, Essex; 19C.

343 Iron balconies, balcony brackets, window guards and railings, stucco terrace; Brighton, Sussex; c. 1815–20.

Iron

There is little iron ore in Britain. Shortage of wood in the 17th century (which also affected glass-making) hampered iron production as copious amounts of charcoal were needed to smelt and forge it, and early attempts to use sea-coal were not very successful. Iron was either wrought, by being hammered into shape or cast in a primitive manner by running the pig-iron (iron too brittle to be wrought) into sand moulds. Early use of iron in buildings was thus restricted to the essential: nails, hinges, and structural rods.

In the 17th century, the arrival in Britain of skilled Huguenot metalworkers such as Jean Tijou demonstrated the potential for decorative ironwork. His wrought-iron gates, screens and balconies in richly curving exuberant three-dimensional patterns was published in 1693 in *A New Booke of Drawings Invented and Desined by John Tijou*. This became a pattern-book for smiths during much of the 18th century. Cast iron became a viable and cheaper alternative once Abraham Darby had simplified the smelting process by substituting charcoal with coke which burnt at a hotter temperature. Isaac Ware pointed out in 1756 that cast iron was 'very serviceable to the builder and a vast expense is saved in many cases by using it (for) rails and balusters it makes a rich and massy appearance when it has cost very little, and wrought iron, much less substantial, would cost a vast sum'.

The cast-iron industry expanded hugely between 1750 and 1820. Foundries were started up strategically close to coal fields and to ports (which imported pig iron) notably Abraham Darby's Coalbrookdale in Shropshire, Wilkinson's in Staffordshire and the Carron Works near Falkirk in Scotland, which produced quantities of railings, gates, fanlights, balconies, window guards, exterior lamps and overthrows — the perfect ornament for the vastly growing number of terraces and villas and an excellent foil to the equally popular stucco. The repertoire of patterns expanded rapidly, many of them becoming standard for decades. A pattern book, first published in 1823 by

344 Wrought-iron entrance gates on stone piers; Frampton-on-Severn, Gloucestershire; 18C.

345 Cast-iron coal plate set in pavement covering shute into coal cellar; Holborn, London; 19C.

346 Gothic Revival iron door furniture on stone terrace; Castle Cary, Somerset; 1876.

347 Art Deco ironwork on glass entrance door and balconies on blocks of flats; Holborn, London; 1930s.

348 Iron window fixture on casement window; Montacute, Somerset.

L. N. Cottingham as *The Ornamental Metalworker's Director*, included pieces in what he termed Grecian, Roman and Gothic styles. Verandas, porches and window canopies were popular early 19th-century additions.

Strictly utilitarian fittings made in cast iron included guttering and down-pipes, ventilation gratings and coal plates (removable covers set into the pavement, enabling coal to be tipped directly into the coal cellar). Cast-iron windows were principally used for warehouses, chapels and schools but were an economic option in the 1820s and 1850s for cottages and almshouses with decorative glazing.

By the Victorian period, cast-iron ornament was becoming far heavier, and linear patterns were giving way to bulky balusters, elaborate scrollwork and dense foliage. Following Pugin's view that construction should not be concealed but 'avowed', door hinges, locks and nails were celebrated in the manner of medieval smiths

349 Overthrow and railings; Wells, Somerset; mid-18C.

350 Railings and drainpipe; Burford, Oxfordshire; 19C.

351 Ironwork bootscraper and niche ornament; Bloomsbury, London; 1770s.

352 Section of continuous iron balcony with Vitruvian scroll on terrace; Belgravia, London; c. 1830 (balcony design 1780s).

353 Gate pier and railings; Notting Hill Gate, London; mid-19C.

354 Exterior lamp and railings on flats; Kensington, London; 1901.

and rendered as 'rich and beautiful decorations'. The Gothic Revival changed the emphasis of ironwork as an exterior feature, as elaborate door ironwork, finials, pennant weathervanes and roof cresting were added to the repertoire of ornaments available to the builder.

The value of cast iron lay in the way it could take ornament, but it was heavy and brittle and, by the end of the 19th century, unfashionable. Repetitive cast ironwork was anathema to adherents of the Arts and Crafts style who wanted metalwork to have a hand-wrought, hammered look. Subsequent manufacturing developments in the iron and steel industry resulted in metal being produced in a wide range of component parts. These became the basis for metalwork on gates, balconies, doors, and finish became more important than ornament. The late 20th-century use of metalwork divided into two streams: the craft-based, and one which explored the use of industrial materials.

355 Balcony over porch; Hampstead Garden Suburb, London; 1930s.

356 Ironwork and its shadow on veranda; Wells, Somerset; early 19C.

357 Garden gate; Dean Village, Edinburgh; 1990s' gate.

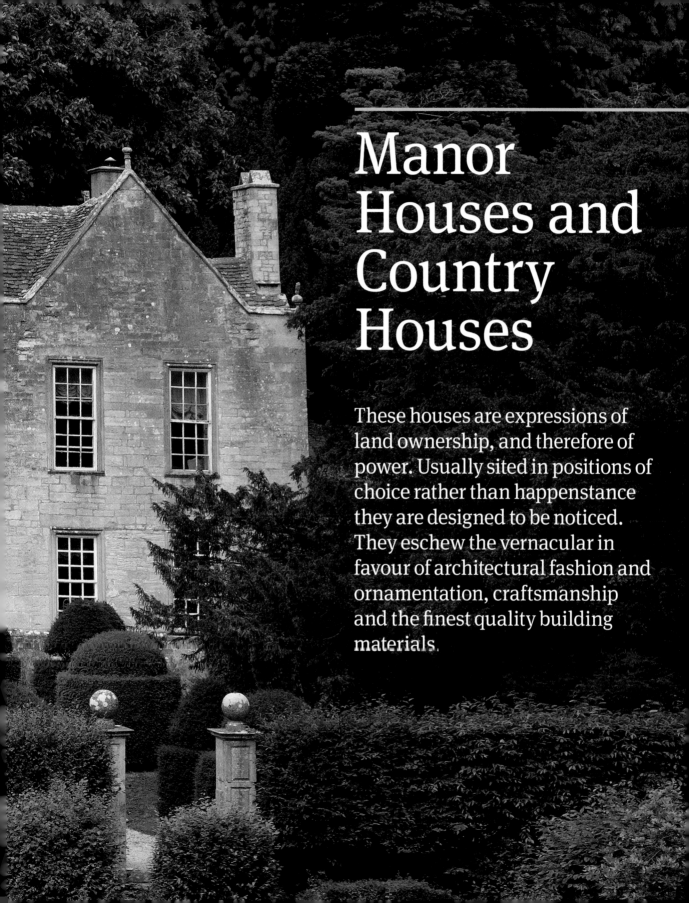

Manor Houses and Country Houses

These houses are expressions of land ownership, and therefore of power. Usually sited in positions of choice rather than happenstance they are designed to be noticed. They eschew the vernacular in favour of architectural fashion and ornamentation, craftsmanship and the finest quality building materials.

Manor Houses and Country Houses

358   359

The manor was the principal administrative unit of the feudal system, and so the earliest part of any original manor house dates from the 12th to 15th centuries. Along with the church the manor house, home to the lord of the manor, was the epicentre of the village. Medieval houses of any importance centred on the great hall where rents were collected, feasts held and justice administered by the manorial court. Some manor houses might be ornamented with turrets or battlements, built not for practical purposes but as a display of power. As well-built houses they usually survived the demise of the feudal system, some remaining in the hands of the same families, some changing hands, but all slowly being added to, improved and modernised by their subsequent owners in accordance with the fluctuations of their fortunes. William Harrison wrote in Holinshed's *Chronicles* of 1577: 'The ancient manors and houses of our gentlemen are yet and for the most part of strong timber, in framing whereof our carpenters have been and are worthily preferred before those of like science among all other nations. Howbeit such as be lately builded are commonly either of brick or hard stone, or both, their rooms large and comely, and houses of office further distant from their lodgings'.

The rich and powerful nobility of the Tudor and Stuart periods expressed their wealth through the building of spectacular houses. As William Harrison pointed out they were 'so magnificent and stately as the basest house of a baron doth often match in our days with some honours of a prince in old time'. In the 18th century the great landowners, increasingly wealthy through the inexorable enclosure of common land and profitability of their estates, took even more enthusiastically to architecture. No longer believing it necessary or desirable to live within the village among their labourers, they proclaimed their status by setting themselves apart. The country seats that they built, competitively large and classically inspired, stood alone in parkland, a carefully contrived picturesque landscape

358 A machiolated castle tower built 1378–80 which survived and became part of a 16C house. Scotney Castle, Kent.

359 Built in the 14C and altered in the 16C this house was until the dissolution of the monasteries the summer residence of the Abbots of Glastonbury, after which it became a farmhouse. Meare, Somerset.

encompassing clumps of trees, distant views and newly formed lakes. To achieve this some landowners obliterated the existing village, and rebuilt it at a distance. Gatehouses and lodges marked the entrances to the demesne with driveways winding sinuously through the park to bring the visitor slowly but impressively to their destination.

The building of large country houses continued through the 19th century and up to the Edwardian period in a progression of styles which proclaimed the culture and taste of the builder. Money was increasingly spent by rich middle-class families, successful in manufacturing, trade and finance, who wished for country houses on a smaller scale from which to follow country pursuits — hunting, shooting and fishing — but had no wish or need to engage in agriculture. After World War I large country house establishments, the upkeep of which had depended upon numerous servants, became increasingly problematic. Demolition or conversion to institutional or commercial use was common, and anxiety over their future existence led to the establishment of the National Trust's Country House Scheme in the 1930s.

366 A country house on a grand and luxurious scale, Waddesdon Manor was built 1874–89 in the French Renaissance style by Baron Ferdinand de Rothschild, who wanted it to house and display his art treasures and to entertain in. The architect was Gabriel-Hippolyte Destailleur who had worked on the restoration of many of the Loire chateaux. Aylesbury, Buckinghamshire.

367 A country house built in 1900, designed by the architect Detmar Blow and combining flint, pebble, brick, thin tiles and thatch in Vernacular or Domestic Revival style. The 'butterfly' ground plan opens out to make the most of the sea view. Happisburgh, Norfolk.

360 Late 14C or early 15C timber-framed medieval manor house. The late 15C gatehouse gives access across the moat. Both this and the gable of the manor have bargeboards carved with foliage. Lower Brockhampton, Herefordshire.

361 Rear elevation of manor house, showing the medieval building to the right and the 1672 addition to the left, both under a roof of Horsham stone slabs. Greatham Manor, Sussex.

362 Entrance front to Cotswold stone manor house begun c.1570 and extended a century later. The gables have ball finials and the mullion windows have dripstones. Kelmscott, Oxfordshire.

363 Façade of house built originally as a hunting lodge, c.1550 by one of Henry VIII's courtiers, an early example of a grand, symmetrical Renaissance-influenced style. The doorway is a pediment supported on fluted pillars.

This would have been only intended as a place to stop and dine. Extended to become a proper country house in the early 17C, and again in the 1790s, a service wing was added in the 1890s — a characteristic history of changing needs. Newark Park, Gloucestershire.

364 A Queen Anne country house, built c.1700 from red brick with grey headers, set behind an 18C brick garden wall. The hipped tile roof has pedimented casement dormer windows and a wooden cornice. Ripe, Sussex.

365 Classical Palladian country house, built 1718–21 to designs by Colen Campbell, featuring four giant fluted Ionic columns supporting a triangular pediment carved with scrolling foliage, a balustrade on the parapet and flanking pavilions. The original small paned sash windows were altered in the 19C to plate glass. Baldersby Park, Yorkshire.

Names and Numbers

In 1765 a bill was passed which required newly built streets to be named and houses numbered. The display of door numbers on all houses became mandatory in London in 1805. On estate villages the cottages were often numbered regardless of position, simply to identify them, and were given plain white ceramic number labels on the door.

In rural communities houses and farms had historically been verbally defined by names which related to their purpose, their ownership, their geography or local landmarks (e.g. Wood Hall, Windmill Farm). The sentimental naming of houses appears to be a notion of the picturesque: Blaise Hamlet built in 1812 had Jessamine, Rose, Vine and Sweet Briar Cottages. Names such as Woodcot introduced the idea of the cottage. The idea became far more elaborate as the century progressed. By using the definite article a suggestion of grandeur was conferred (e.g. The Elms, The Towers). Victorian Gothic Revival houses were frequently given names which suggested antiquity such as The Chantry or The Grange, and such names frequently appear cut into the gate piers.

While detached houses first claimed a right to a name, terrace houses soon followed suit, even though they had a statutory number as well. Often a plaque was incorporated into the design of the façade so that the owner could have the house name added if they wished. Alternatives included gilded lettering on fanlights or even coloured leaded glass. Favourite early themes were royalty (Victoria, Albert, Adelaide, Alexandra); great houses (Cliveden, Chatsworth, Hardwick); place names representing favourite destinations, birthplaces or just exotic faraway lands (St Kitts, Lamorna); combinations of pleasant associations (Sunnybank, Meadowview, Rose Villa).

368 Carved stone plaque on Clarence Cottage; Regent's Park, London; early 19C.

369 Suspended wooden sign over front porch (Thirlmere); Writtle, Essex; 1930s.

370 Carved stone Gothic Revival gate pier (The Tower); Hampstead, London; c. 1870.

368	370	371	372
369	373	374	375
			376

With the burgeoning of the suburbs naming took on a greater significance in the desire to emphasise individuality and, critically, ownership. On a practical level house names were often needed for identification until the local authority adopted the road and instigated a formal numbering. At this point the naming of houses was even extended to Hollywood stars (Barrymore), jokes (Haventwedonewell) or combined Christian names (Brymoy).

371 Cast metal plaque on gate pier (Laburnum); Modbury, Devon; late 19C.

372 Painted glass on door light (Parliament Hill Mansions); Kentish Town, London; c. 1890.

373 Arts and Crafts gilded lettering on front door (Garden Corner); Chelsea, London; 1906.

374 Incised plaque set on wall of house (Hardwicke); Chelmsford, Essex; 1915.

375 Screw-on DIY plastic letters on metal gate, (Kuala Lumpur); Eel Pie Island, London; 1960s.

376 Art Deco keystone over entrance to block of flats (Number 50); Knightsbridge, London; 1930s.

Paint

As exterior surfaces are in constant need of being recoated, paint is usually an ephemeral detail. Primarily its purpose is to protect (wood and iron have always needed paint treatments to prevent rot and rust), but paint can also ornament, decorate and express individuality.

Early lead-based paint was coloured with earth pigments: browns, greys, off-whites, dull greens, red ochre and black. During the 18th century it was recommended that gates and railings should be 'invisible' green; window sashes were often stone coloured, and front doors favoured a dark colour. Cream was the favourite colour of the late 19th century, while bright white became a 20th-century classic. Brick and stone were never intended to be painted, although roughly built stone cottages were often whitewashed for extra impermeability. Renders all lent themselves to colour washes: the traditional method was limewash, some areas becoming associated with particular shades, such as 'Suffolk pink'. Originally stucco was intended to mimic the colour of stone with the rustication emphasised by darker paintwork to give a far darker result than is expected today.

The development of fast, chemically based colours during the second half of the 19th century vastly widened the choices, and it cost no more to paint something in a bright colour than in the more traditional hues. Easy access to colour also gave people the ability to differentiate themselves from their neighbours. One author wrote in 1924 that despite the shortage of money for building materials one now had 'the sudden astonishing discovery of colour' (*The Smaller House* published by Architectural Press) which gave a house added interest at no extra cost. (He suggested primrose roughcast with jade green paintwork.) Strong exterior colours were revived in the 1960s, a period notorious for challenging historical correctness. By the end of the century authentic period colours were made commercially available by the heritage industry.

377	380	381
378	382	383
379	384	385
	386	

377 Maroon paint on early 18C terrace; Spitalfields, London.

378 Yellow ochre limewash on estate cottage; Badminton, Gloucestershire.

379 Red-painted brick, 1950s end-of-terrace house; Stevenage New Town, Hertfordshire.

380 Multi-coloured individual façades on mid-19C terrace; Kentish Town, London.

381 Rendered cottage painted with trompe-l'oeil heavy stone blocks; Kirkmichael, Ayrshire.

382 Pink colour-washed 15C hall house with later additions; Easthorpe, Essex.

383 Green and yellow paint on rendered cottage; Fishguard, Pembrokeshire.

384 Red paint and black creosote on seaside summer bungalow; Southwold, Suffolk.

385 Blue painted early 19C terrace; Highgate, London.

386 Dividing colour line on stone terrace, dated 1764 on lintel; Garlieston, Dumfries and Galloway.

Paths and Drives

In a front garden of any size there is a need for a clear path to the front door, and in many cases a historic alternative route to the back door or tradesman's entrance. The pattern is usually set by the style of architecture: thus the formal, four-square house, designed with a central doorway, would have a straight path leading directly up to it. However, as soon as a house had an asymmetrical façade, the path could be correspondingly serpentine. The planting of the garden frequently emphasised these features. Equally the status of the house could be immediately apparent from the existence of a carriage drive — a feature subsequently adapted for the car. While the detached garage was a clear successor to the coach house, the notion of the integral garage which appeared in the second decade of the 20th century led to a revised planning of paths and entrances.

Until skirts ceased to sweep the ground, the laying of terraces, cobbles and gravel walks was an important consideration; unmetalled roads and horse-traffic contributed to an unpleasant muddiness that had to be avoided. Tiled paths were a perfect urban solution as they met the criteria of being both ornamental and practical. Crazy paving, like rockeries and cinder walling, was also typical of the early 20th century, and characteristic of a period that sought to create good effects out of waste products. Later, clean, modern, minimalist effects were created with materials such as bonded gravel, slate and large pebbles. The noise made from walking on pebbles was considered an added security factor.

The advent of ready-mixed concrete and tarmacadam led to the creation of many gloomy paths and drives, and perhaps contributed to the nostalgia for the timeless vision of the flower-bordered cottage path.

387 Cottage garden path; Little Missenden, Buckinghamshire.

388 Slate path and loose pebbles; Chelsea, London; 1990s.

387	389 390 391
388	392 393 394 395

389 Entrance with pond, steps and ramp; Blackheath, London; 1968.

390 Curved sweep for car to front of house; Putney, London; 1930s.

391 Drive to garage and side path to house; Sutton, Surrey; 1920s.

392 Curving path of encaustic tile on terrace; Cardiff; 1920s.

393 Stone paving to stone terrace; New Town, Edinburgh; early 19C.

394 Brick house with brick path; Stedham, Sussex; early 18C house, modern path.

395 Hedge with clipped castellations bordering concrete path; Aston Rowant, Oxfordshire.

Porches

For practical reasons the porch has always been seen as more of a necessity in the country. Traditionally it was a place where people could wait to be let into the house. At its simplest it consisted of slabs of stone to keep the rain off the door, and at its most complex the porch was a weatherproof space used for a multitude of purposes, providing a buffer between inside and out. Porches served to retain warmth inside the house as well as providing a neutral zone where deliveries could be safely left or collections made. During the 16th and 17th centuries the gabled porch was a significant feature, often built to double height with a decorative window above the entrance.

One early 19th-century author wrote that a vicarage should be built with an open porch as a welcome to the poor (P. F. Robinson, *Village Architecture*), and this detail was certainly frequently seen as an extension of the hospitality of the house as well as a practical adjunct.

Cottage porches may seem to be a picturesque cliché but they were frequently essential places to work, offering shelter and a light area in a cottage that was often dark and cold. They were usually made from local materials, thatched or tiled, often consciously rustic using rough poles rather than sawn timber. One of the enduring porch patterns, the trellis — in wood, wire-work or ironwork — had a practical application as a support for climbing plants. William Morris built deep sitting porches at Red House in Bexleyheath, facing into the garden, as places to talk and sew.

The porch was an important feature of the suburban house, a way of emphasizing individuality and identifying it as a move away from the featureless urban terrace. At the turn of the 20th century, rather than an outwards projection, the porch space tended to be recessed in from the façade.

396 Double-storey gabled timber-frame porch; Potterne, Wiltshire; late 15C.

397 Double-storey gabled brick porch; Abinger Hammer, Surrey; c. 1660.

398 Rustic woodwork porch with twig mosaic; Stedham, Sussex; 19C.

| 396 | | 398 | 399 | 400 | 401 |
| 397 | | 402 | 403 | 404 | 405 |

399 Glass and iron canopy; Bayswater, London; house c.1840, porch later addition.

400 Ironwork porch on stone house; Corton, Wiltshire; early 19C.

401 Stucco porch on terrace; Belgravia, London; c.1840.

402 Covered-in porch with coloured glass and slate roof on row of cottages; Kingsbridge, Devon; late 19C.

403 Wood and brick porch with coloured glass and house name in gable; Clapham, London; 1890s.

404 Weatherboarded double-storey porch on terrace; Hampstead Garden Suburb, London; 1909.

405 Brick and glass porch; Stevenage New Town, Hertfordshire; 1955–57.

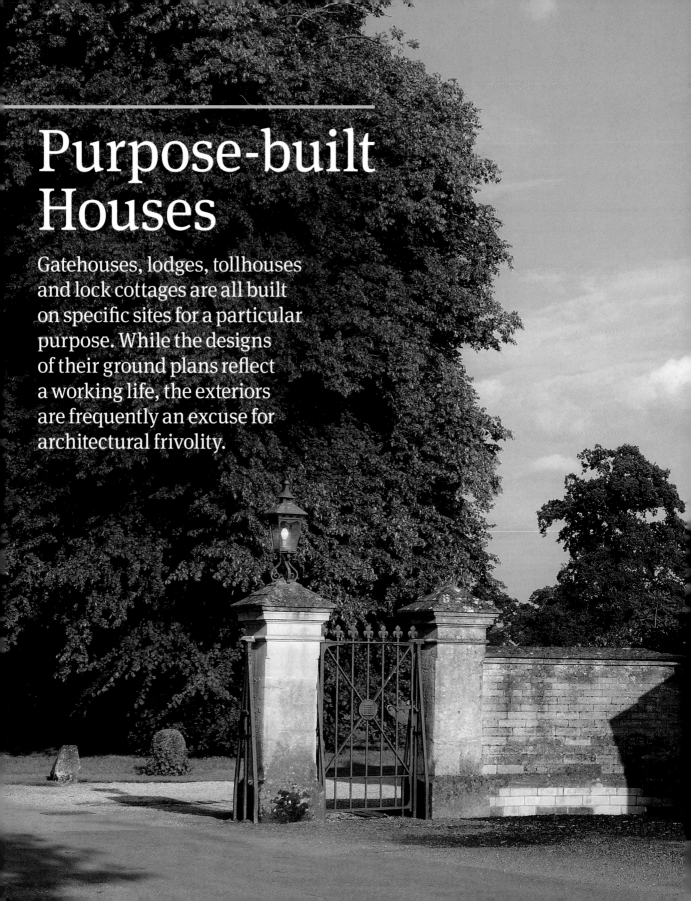

Purpose-built Houses

Gatehouses, lodges, tollhouses and lock cottages are all built on specific sites for a particular purpose. While the designs of their ground plans reflect a working life, the exteriors are frequently an excuse for architectural frivolity.

Purpose-built Houses

The siting and appearance of various types of British houses are connected to a specific purpose. A job needed doing, and the worker needed to live *in situ*. Guardianship is the common theme in these dwellings: the gatehouse or lodge monitors an entrance; a tollhouse watches road traffic; a lock-keeper's cottage oversees a canal; a railway cottage surveys a crossing point.

The notion of a gatehouse derives from castle architecture where a fortified and castellated drawbridge entrance protected the space within. This gave rise to the crenellations, battlements, turrets, machicolations and arrow loops that remained part of the ornamental vocabulary for many gatehouses well into the 19th century, by which time boiling oil and longbows were very distant history. In the 14th century abbeys, cathedral closes, bishop's palaces, monasteries, colleges and nobles' houses had adopted the gatehouse entrance. Sometimes, as at Cleve Abbey, it doubled as lodgings for visitors. But by the late Tudor period, although the need to fortify was past, the gatehouse remained a feature of larger houses. These were often exercises in ostentation, such as the elaborate high brick structures of Layer Marney in Essex or Sissinghurst in Kent. Heraldic crests and coats of arms were prominent, further declaration of the family's status. The parkland that encircled large country houses in the 18th century was marked as an elite refuge by the addition of an impressive entrance. A popular choice was based on the classical triumphal arch, which could house a gatekeeper on either side.

A simpler alternative was the lodge cottage. Built as an eye-catcher this would always be in a distinctive architectural style, either echoing the main house or creating a picturesque point in the landscape. A number of pattern books, such as Thomas Dearn's *Designs for Lodges and Entrances to Parks, Paddocks and Pleasure Grounds, in the Gothic, Cottage and Fancy Styles* (1811) provide alternatives in a full range of styles from gothic to classical, or using

406 Tollhouse facing in three directions, each marked with a bargeboarded gable. Built c.1831 when Bruton Turnpike took over new road to Frome. Bruton, Somerset.

407 Gatehouse to Charlecote, built c. 1560 of brick and stone. Two octagonal turrets stand at either corner of the front façade. Charlecote, Warwickshire.

408 Octagonal tollhouse on the Plymouth and Tavistock Turnpike, built c. 1822 with cladding of local slate. Tavistock, Devon.

the picturesque vocabulary of bargeboards, trellis porches, fancy glazing and twisted chimneys. The Victorians too built lodges, often replacing whimsy by gravitas expressed by an impressive show of defensive spiky ironwork. Caretakers at schools, hospitals, asylums, cemeteries, hospitals and public parks were housed in lodges.

Tollhouses date from the turnpike road system which lasted from 1663 and 1835 and radically improved conditions of travel until the arrival of the railways. Tolls were paid for passing sections of road, and the money collected enabled the turnpike trusts who owned the roads to pay for their upkeep. Accommodation was needed for the toll collector and his family, who had to guard the road at all times and in all weathers. Although many tollhouses were similar in design to lodges, they had some specific features. They were situated at strategic pinch points in the road and abutted directly onto it to prevent toll-dodging. Since it was important that the pikeman could easily see oncoming traffic, the tollhouse often had projecting polygonal porches or was circular in shape, with large windows. The tollhouse's size would relate to the importance of the road, but in the main they were well-built in keeping with the responsibility of the job. The unpopularity of toll-collecting with the travelling public, and the relatively large sums of money garnered, led to a sometimes castellated, fortified architectural style. Many trusts favoured the 'gothick', in vogue during the early 19th century.

Of shorter time span were the boom canal-building years, lasting from the 1790s to 1830s. Canal companies supplied cottages for toll clerks, lock-keepers, bridgemen and lengthsmen (responsible for the upkeep of a specific stretch of waterway). Similar in style and purpose to toll cottages some companies had a uniform look: for its lock-keepers' cottages, the Shropshire Union used a pattern of yellow brick with a polygonal bay front which had been designed by Thomas Telford for his Holyhead Road tollhouses.

409 Gate lodge to the County Lunatic Asylum, built in Jacobean Revival style with shaped gables and an ogee-domed turret. The finials on this and the gables are in the form of a mace, perhaps in reference to the custodial nature of the main building, c. 1850. South Horrington, Somerset.

410 Victorian stone gate lodge with decorative bargeboards and bay window facing the thoroughfare, the entrance marked by highly elaborate cast-iron railings and gate piers. Larne, Co. Antrim.

411 Scottish baronial-style lodge with turret and crow-step gables to Cally House. Gatehouse of Fleet, Dumfries and Galloway.

412 Lock-keeper's cottage on the Llangollen canal, brick with a bowed front and slate roofed veranda, c. 1810. Near Acton, Cheshire.

413 Gate lodge built in 1809 as *cottage orné*, in polygonal form with central chimney, the thatching dipping down to create an umbrella effect. The rustic poles of the porch are a typical feature of the style. Hinton Martell, Dorset.

414 Tollhouse built c. 1830–40 for the Melksham Turnpike Trust, single-storey ashlar stone in Tudor Revival style with stone mullion windows and arched doorway. The central canted bay looks out in two directions. Box, Wiltshire.

415 Picturesque castle-style cottage built c. 1800 for the fish keeper employed by Logan House, who guarded the stock of fresh fish in the salt water pond on the rocks below. Port Logan, Dumfries and Galloway.

Rainwater Heads and Drainpipes

416 Lead downpipe and fixing, cast with heraldic scallop shell and initials; Stanway House, Chipping Campden, Gloucestershire; 16C.

It is recorded that lead downpipes were ordered for the White Tower of the Tower of London in 1240 to prevent rainwater spoiling the whitewashed walls. The usual medieval solution — frequently seen on church architecture and presumably adapted for domestic use — was a gargoyle that projected the water away from the wall. Square-section lead downpipes usually with box-shaped heads at roof level subsequently became a decorative feature of substantial Elizabethan and Jacobean houses. Since lead was easily cast, it often proved irresistible to include some ornament either placed on the rainwater head or the horizontal fixing points: usually dates, monograms, crests and heraldic motifs. These presumably often matched lead cisterns which collected water at ground level.

After the Great Fire downpipes were required in London according to new regulations instituted in 1667. In 1763 an Act of Parliament demanded that downpipes be included on new housing which by this time could be manufactured in cast iron, and rainwater heads became a more efficient cup-shape. On houses built in the Italianate style with markedly projecting eaves the gutter became integral to the cornice and was often supported on double brackets. The sight of rainwater heads and downpipes was eliminated as far as possible on Classical façades, and they were certainly not considered an opportunity for ornament.

In the 19th century roof silhouettes reverted to steeper and more complicated profiles and there was a corresponding need for well-articulated systems of gutters and downpipes. These were sometimes appropriately decorated with Gothic motifs such as castellated rainwater heads and Tudor roses. The Victorian enthusiasm for seeking out appropriate ornament produced rainwater heads embossed with watery motifs such as bulrushes, dolphins and boats. Plastic guttering in the 20th century appears to have made little stylistic contribution to this detail.

417 Downpipe system; Drumlanrig Castle, Dumfries and Galloway; 1680–90.

418 Painted cast-iron gutter, rainwater head and downpipe on terrace; Morningside, Edinburgh; 1878.

419 Lead rainwater head and downpipe; Canons Ashby, Northamptonshire; 1706.

420 Painted lead rainwater head; Uley, Gloucestershire; 1743.

421 Painted cast-iron rainwater head and downpipe: Great Easton, Essex; 1848.

422 Painted lead downpipe and fixing, cast with heraldic crest; Burton Agnes Hall, Yorkshire; early 17C.

423 Lead downpipe fixing, cast with Arts and Crafts plant motif; Lythe, North Yorkshire; 1890s.

424 Painted cast-iron rainwater head with fish motif; Port Sunlight, Cheshire; c. 1900.

425 Painted cast-iron rainwater head in form of Art Deco urn; Castle Cary, Somerset; 1930s.

Renderings

Rendering a building was done for a variety of reasons: weather-proofing, draughtproofing or fireproofing. It was an essential finish to a cob building as without it the walls were liable to disintegrate. Renders covered cheap or unfashionable building materials with a smooth and cohesive finish, e.g. on inferior bricks, rubblestone or a stone too hard to work to a fine finish. They were often a later addition.

Roughcast or harling (the term usually used in Scotland and Ireland) added small stones, grit, and even shells to the wet plaster mixture and then applied it to the walls, giving a softer effect than pebbledash where the dry pebbles were thrown at the wet plaster.

During the second half of the 18th century, in an attempt to make houses look as Classical as possible (and by association built of stone), there was much experimentation with covering bricks with plaster, known as stucco, in imitation of fine stone blocks. Once a successful formula was discovered it was widely used and whole terraces of houses were stuccoed giving impressively unified results. Parker's Roman Cement, patented in 1796, was the first stucco that could be relied on not to fall off in a short space of time. This was improved upon by Joseph Aspdin's Portland Cement (patented in 1824) which was stronger. Defining selected areas of brick with smooth cement, for example around windows, doorcases, porches or to form quoins and rustication, became a popular form of decoration in Victorian building.

Arts and Crafts-style builders were looking for a texture that looked honest, workmanlike and rural and thus favoured roughcast. By contrast, the Modernists of the 1930s favoured a clean, white concrete finish that looked smoothly mechanical. Pebbledash became synonymous with the ubiquitous style of suburban housing. Rendering of all types also provided a surface for colour.

426 Harling on Scottish Baronial wing of house; Lunga, Argyll; 18C/19C.

427 Stucco terrace; Regent's Park, London; 1825.

426		428		429
427		430	431 432	433

428 Smooth cement render on Modern Movement house; Dartington, Devon; 1935.

429 Arts and Crafts roughcast on terrace; Letchworth Garden City, Hertfordshire; 1912.

430 Pebbledash on modified suburban house; Colchester, Essex; 1930s (date of alterations unknown).

431 Cement render striped with brick on terrace; Kensington, London; 1883.

432 Early pebbledash with ornamental timber-framing on estate cottage; Albury, Surrey; 1850s.

433 Refurbished tower block; Deptford, London; late 1960s block, late 20C refurbishment.

Roofs

Battlements, or crenellations, the emblem of fortification, state that an Englishman's home is indeed his castle. In the 12th century battlements were only licensed to certain nobles, such was their perceived symbolic power; later, crenellations took on a lesser, decorative or mock-heroic role.

The magnificent timber roof structures of early houses were reflected in a gabled outline and steeply pitched roofs. With the advent of Classicism, it was replaced by a flat four-square line. During the late 16th and early 17th centuries some of the grandest houses had impressively fashionable skylines: pierced strapwork, obelisks and finials. In a Classical façade the emphasis was on the cornice, but options included a cupola, balustrade or pediment. The pitch of the roof gradually diminished from the high-hipped examples of the late 17th century to the shallow forms of the early 19th.

Steeply pitched roofs were perceived as picturesque and were revived in the 19th century, their roofline often further decorated with fancy ridge tiles or weather vanes. Victorian eclecticism also embraced the French Second Empire style, characterised by a mansard roof combined with elaborate ironwork cresting. The later Arts and Crafts style featured deep roofs, sometimes including catslides which came below porch level. Deep roofs were, however, uneconomic and cheaper housing adopted a more minimalist approach.

The turret, originally a medieval look-out point, was an essential feature of Scottish architecture and also frequently reappears in the 19th century, a favourite motif for corner or end-of-terrace houses. The flat roof was an innovation of the Modern Movement, influenced by Le Corbusier's work for hotter climates where it provided space for

434 Brick castellated stair tower; Ingatestone Hall, Essex; c. 1540.

435 Stone hipped roof; Uley, Gloucestershire; early 18C.

open-air activity. The British climate, however, meant that puddles were a more usual sight on flat roofs, and they were always treated with suspicion. Contemporary alternatives of the 1950s and 1960s experimented with monopitch and asymmetrical roofs. More recently the development of flexible roofing material in profile metal has produced a new range of curved roofs.

436 Balustrade on stucco terrace; Winchester, Hampshire, c. 1840.

437 Pitched roof on semi-detached villa; Cardiff; late 19C.

438 Catslide roof on Arts and Crafts terrace; Letchworth Garden City, Hertfordshire; c.1906.

439 Flat roof on cement-rendered house; Frinton-on-Sea, Essex; 1930s.

440 Monopitch roof on linked housing; Ditcheat, Somerset; 1960s.

441 Curved profile metal roof; Kentish Town, London; 1993.

442 Carved stone cresting for Elizabeth Shrewsbury; Hardwick Hall, Derbyshire; 1590–1610.

443 Cupola with bell and weathervane on almshouses; Wootton-under-Edge, Gloucestershire; 1727.

444 Cast-iron roof cresting on terrace; Crouch End, London; c. 1890.

445 Tower with loggia and turrets; Hampstead, London; c. 1870.

446 Carved stone finials and decorative chimneys (remaining summerhouse of Campden House); Chipping Campden, Gloucestershire; c. 1613.

447 Galley-shaped weathervane; Highgate, London; c. 1928.

448 Clay ridge tiles; Wedmore, Somerset; c. 1840.

449 Pinnacle and polygonal turret on terrace; Hampstead, London; early 20C.

450 Turret, rendered in harling; Traquair House, Scottish Borders; 17C.

451 Decoratively thatched roof ridge on cottage; New Forest, Hampshire.

442	443 444	446	447 448
	445	449 450	451

Roofing Materials

452 Barley-straw thatch weighted with stones on croft; Outer Hebrides; Western Isles.

453 Thatch on timber-frame cottage; Hatfield Broad Oak, Essex.

Reed, straw, heather, brushwood and broom were among the materials used for thatching. Banned on London houses in 1212 as a fire risk (a precaution subsequently followed in other places) thatching methods survived by tradition but were gradually replaced by longer-lasting materials. By World War II thatching was a near-extinct skill, but the 1970s' craft revival led to a reinvention of decorative effects. From the 14th century stone slates were used for roofing. Generally lighter and smaller, limestone tiles were more flexible for roof structures with steep pitches, while sandstone was used on shallower pitches to create simpler roof shapes. In the pre-industrial period plain rectangular tiles, together with shaped tiles for ridges and valley gutters, were made from local clay. The Victorians contributed fancy scale and scalloped shapes and colours in their desire for all-over ornamentation.

Larger and lighter pantiles were used from the 17th century, particularly in regions exposed to Dutch influence. In the early 18th century local manufacturers revealed regional peculiarities, e.g. glazed black pantiles in Norfolk. So-called Roman tiles were similar to pantiles but with a different profile, and manufactured on large scale in Somerset — instead of the S-curve tubular ridges run from top to bottom; variations include double or triple Romans (two or three ridges). Brightly coloured green- or blue-glazed pantiles were fashionably different in the 1920s and 1930s. Concrete versions of most kinds of tile were manufactured in the 20th century.

Slate is a natural, light roofing material light, easily split and impervious to frost. The Welsh slate industry was developed by Lord Penrhyn in the 1760s. Initially slate was often used where it was less visible but by the middle of the 19th century it had become the standard roofing material. Shortages of money and materials after

World War I led to experimentation with cheap roofing materials such as asbestos tiles (which were criticised for their pink colour), corrugated iron (too hot and noisy) and tarred felt. Popular for bungalows and holiday houses, some districts nevertheless forbade the use of such alien materials.

452	454	455	456
453	457	458	
	459	460	

454 Stone slates; Stanley Pontlarge, Gloucestershire; 14C and later (house).

455 Tile roof on brick farmhouse; Appledore, Kent; 17C.

456 Scallop-shaped slate tiles on Chatsworth estate cottage; Edensor, Derbyshire; 1830s.

457 Slate roof; model terrace housing for miners; New Bolsover, Derbyshire; 1888–93.

458 Black-glazed pantiles with flint and brick; Beccles, Norfolk; 17C.

459 Triple roman clay tiles on stone cottage; Ditcheat, Somerset.

460 Mansard roof with green-glazed pantiles on brick house; Welwyn Garden City, Hertfordshire; late 1920s–early 1930s.

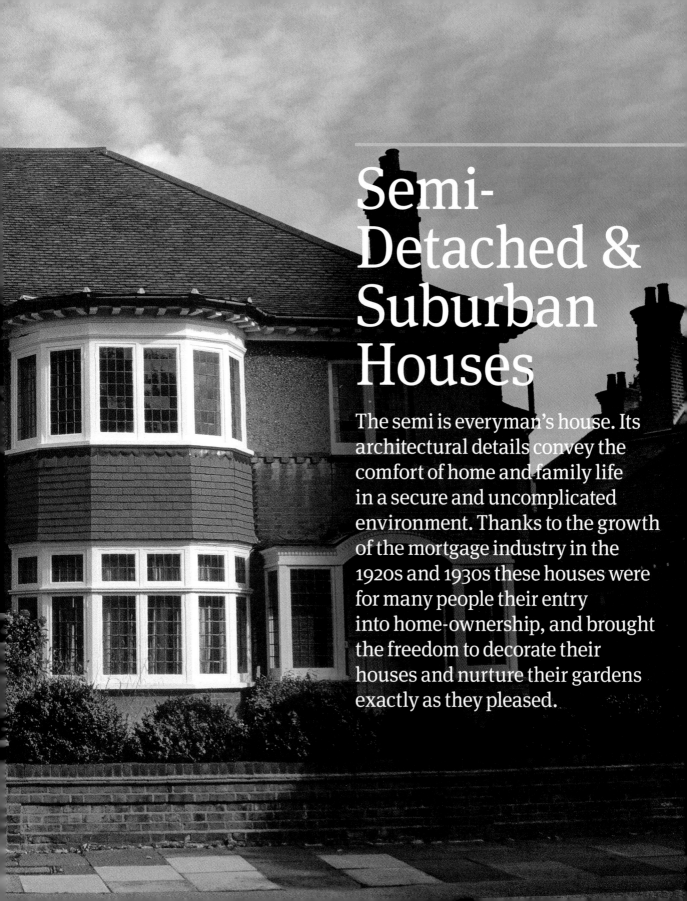

Semi-Detached & Suburban Houses

The semi is everyman's house. Its architectural details convey the comfort of home and family life in a secure and uncomplicated environment. Thanks to the growth of the mortgage industry in the 1920s and 1930s these houses were for many people their entry into home-ownership, and brought the freedom to decorate their houses and nurture their gardens exactly as they pleased.

Semi-detached & Suburban Houses

For the aspirational mid-Victorian, a detached house in suburbia was the ideal; but he might have to compromise on a house that was semi-detached. The semi-detached house, which had been used from the early 18th century as an economic way of housing agricultural workers, was an increasingly popular solution in the suburbs for the same reason. The exodus from town was attractive from the mid-Victorian period onwards, as cities became increasingly crowded and polluted. The suburbs, although never fashionable, offered fresh air and convenience.

A very early use of the term appears in *The Semi-Detached House*, an 1859 novel by Emily Eden which takes place in the imaginary London suburb of Dulham. It opens with Blanche, the wife of an ambitious young diplomat, who does not feel that Pleasance — as the house is called — is her rightful milieu: 'The only fault of the house is that it is semi-detached.... Oh, Aunt Sarah! You don't mean that you expect me to live in a semi-detached house?' she complains. E. L. Blackburne's *Suburban and Rural Architecture* (1867) offered an eclectic range of styles (French or English Gothic, Italian or German) for suburban semi-detached houses. He noted that they met 'the great requirement of a suburban residence, viz: as much accommodation as possible at minimum expense'. More spacious than a terrace and attached to only one neighbour, it could, at first glance, appear as a single impressive villa residence.

Suburbia has always been an ever-changing zone: for example in London city merchants moved out to Islington in the 1790s for a suburban quality of life. Bedford Park, built in the 1880s, was considered Britain's first proper suburb because it was designed with its own amenities, and it became an area that in the 1920s would have seemed positively metropolitan to the residents of Purley and Pinner. The semi-detached house came into its own from the early 20th century onwards, as the form suited modern ideas about suburban

461 Late Victorian or early Edwardian semi-detached house built facing the sea with balconies and double-height bay windows. Near Bideford, Devon.

462 A pair of brick semi-detached villas with stucco details c.1840 in De Beauvoir Town. The architect, W.C. Lockner, planned the spacious square and streets over 130 acres. Hackney, East London.

463 Two detached Arts and Crafts style houses designed by Michael Bunney built c. 1910 in Hampstead Garden Suburb the layout of which took into consideration natural features and contours. Hedged front gardens were mandatory. North London.

living. Ebenezer Howard's theories of the Garden City movement realised at Letchworth were also influential: he believed that houses should also be surrounded by their own gardens and this was easily and cheaply achieved with semi-detached houses. However, his idea that work and home should be in close proximity has never been so easily achieved by the suburbanite.

Fashionable architectural features were derived from the vernacular of the Arts and Crafts movement, so tile hanging, gables, terra-cotta ornament, fretwork porches, bay windows and turrets appear on suburban houses built along new winding avenues and cul-de-sacs. The expansion in public transport — buses, underground and railway — made swathes of countryside easily accessible for those working in town and city, and construction companies were competing to build houses on it.

The growth of the suburbs which started in the early part of the 20th-century exploded in the interwar years when around four million new houses were built. The majority of these were semi-detached, bought by a new class of house-owner on easy terms. Developers contrived to provide individuality by offering 'traditional' variations of mock Tudor half-timbering, coloured glass depicting galleons and sunsets in front doors and hall windows, pebbledash rendering and waney-edged weatherboarding. The alternative 'moderne' style

464 An archetypical semi-detached 1930s house that could have been built anywhere in the British Isles. It has the key features of ornamental timber framing in the gables, tile hanging and a recessed porch. Ilkley, Yorkshire.

464	
465	468
466 467	469
	470

comprised white rendered walls, steel 'suntrap' windows and bright green or blue glazed pantiles. Novelist Frank Swinnerton described the semi-detached-dwelling commuter in 1926: 'The typical suburban has his pipe, his morning and evening newspapers, his tea-shop lunch, his strip of garden, his local tennis, football and cricket clubs... his gramophone, his wireless set. He has developed great skill in the manipulation of motor engines and electric lights. He is sometimes an amateur carpenter; he sometimes studies courses which are to bring him better memory, better work, and invariably better wages'.

The association of the suburbs with a better life continued up to the beginning of World War II: 'Live in the sun and tonic air of a Morrell Estate' stated a 1935 advertisement for houses in suburban Kent: 14 shillings and 8 pence a week for a semi-detached house with lounge, dining room, kitchen, three bedrooms and tiled bathroom. Surburban estates of detached and semi-detached houses, built at the edge of towns and cities by both local authorities and private developers, continued to be a feature in the post-war landscape, but the increasing dependence on the car removed the inclusion of local amenities that had been a feature of earlier suburbs.

465 1920s house. The cladding of waney-edge boarding was a popular feature of the period and intended to lend a rustic and domestic air. The addition of shutters is probably later, alterations and improvements being a continual element in suburban house ownership. Bromley, Kent.

466 Detached suburban house with a distinctive brickwork doorway and arched central window setting it apart from its neighbours. Light green paintwork against white painted walls was an extremely fashionable combination in the late 1920s and early 1930s. Winchmore Hill, North London.

467 A pair of detached mock-Tudor suburban houses built along a main road, featuring oriel windows with leaded casements and first-floor jetties. Norwood, South London.

468 Modernist houses with flat roofs, plain white walls, balconies and metal windows were never as popular during the interwar period as variations on mock Tudor or vernacular. An integral garage is unusual at this date and decidedly modern. Frinton-on-Sea, Essex.

469 Monopitch and asymmetrical roofs were an adventurous addition of the 1960s, as in this small detached house. The picture window in the front is frosted at lower level. Waterlooville, Hampshire.

470 Large detached 1960s suburban house showing the influence of the American suburbs with a double integral garage and an open front garden. The use of sections of vertical wood cladding and textured stone are typical of the period. Barnton, Edinburgh.

Stone

471 Banded limestone and flint; Maiden Newton, Dorset.

472 Reconstituted stone; Uley, Gloucestershire; 1992.

Building in stone has always been prestigious, reflecting the amount of effort involved in producing a stone wall (far greater than timber-framing or brick). As a building material, stone has the advantage of being recyclable, as lintels, carvings, door and window frames were often re-used from one building to the next. Most stone houses in Britain have been built from whatever was locally quarried, giving domestic architecture an immense range of colours and textures. In brief the main types are:

Limestone (specific names include Portland, Ham, Colleyweston, Bath, Kentish rag, but also includes chalk and lias. Chalk as a building stone is sometimes referred to as clunch). This occurs in bands stretching from the south-west to the north-east. Some is very good for carving and it is used for both walls and roofing.

Sandstone (includes Yorkshire gritstone, Horsham, Red sandstone, carstone greensand and millstone grit) varies in colour and is quarried patchily all over Britain. Available in much larger blocks than limestone, it cannot however be carved to the same crispness.

Granite is the hardest building stone and therefore most difficult to work. It is used particularly in north-eastern Scotland, Cornwall and Cumbria.

Flints occur in chalk and are used mainly in East Anglia and in southern coastal areas where there is little other local stone. They are used in their natural cobble shape or split (knapped) and sometimes squared, and because of their size have to be used with brick or stone for corner-building.

Other forms include *pudding-stone* (a natural aggregate); *slate* from north-west and mid-Wales, the Lake District and Cornwall, which splits into slabs and tiles and was thus only suitable for roofing and cladding. There is virtually no *marble* present in Britain, but the description is given to extremely hard limestone such as *Purbeck marble*.

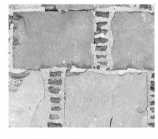

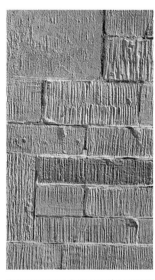

471		473 474
472		475 476 477 478
		479 480

473 Sandstone with granite snecking; Port William, Dumfries and Galloway.

474 Knapped flint; Beccles, Suffolk.

475 Sandstone; Dumfries, Dumfries and Galloway.

476 Carstone with galletting; Denver, Norfolk.

477 Flint cobbles and painted brick; Brighton, Sussex.

478 Ashlar limestone; Woodchester, Gloucestershire.

479 Granite; Leith, Edinburgh.

480 Lias limestone with ammonite; Evercreech, Somerset.

Stone Carving

Carved stone detail was used to express quality and prestige, and to create fashion in architectural style. It has also been used to personalise a house by the addition of carved stone gate piers with heraldic devices and crests, and by plaques with initials and dates. The skills of early stonemasons were honed on churches, but many motifs could also be found in domestic architecture: masks, corbel stones, finials or gothic tracery. Builders during the Tudor and Jacobean period were passionately addicted to ornamentation and included as much carving as possible anywhere that it would fit, as finials, labels, or cresting. By contrast, 17th- and 18th-century Classicism designated specific areas for carved ornament: capitals on columns and pilasters, door and window surrounds, pediments, quoins, rustication and keystones. Isaac Ware warned: 'Take care in proportion, or they cease to be ornaments: they are loads and patches upon the face of the building, and seem not to belong'.

During the 19th century the increased use of steam saws, hammers and mobile cranes made stone a far more accessible commodity. The Gothic Revival, combined with mechanisation, led to an explosion of carved decoration, much of it in the naturalistic tradition. Quarries supplied sections of carved stone for window frames, balustrades, cornices, doorways and porches that could be ordered from their catalogues. Victorian builders' catalogues also advertised a number of artificial stones such as Ransome's Patent Concrete Stone (an 'admixture of sand and chalk with silicate of soda pressed into moulds or blocks and afterwards saturated with a solution of chloride of calcium'), Patent Victoria Stone, or Syenitic Stone. Materials such as these were made into gate finials, urns, balustrades or ornamental door or window heads. By the end of World War I superfluous stone ornament had become both unfashionable and economically unviable.

481 Detail from porch with strapwork and mask; Audley End, Essex; early 17C.

482 Grotesque head keystone over sash window; Bristol; 1709–11.

481	483 484
482	485 486
	487 488 489 490

483 Vermiculated rustication on gatehouse; Fonthill, Tisbury, Wiltshire; mid-18C.

484 Keystone on doorway; Cardiff; c. 1900.

485 Entablature and Corinthian capital; Queen Square, Bath; 1728.

486 House name plaque with date and owner's initials; Evercreech, Somerset; 1899.

487 Porch and decorated window surround; Sherborne, Dorset; late 18C.

488 Entablature and emblem; The Circus, Bath; 1754.

489 Carved doorcase; Queen Square, Bath; c. 1730.

490 Frieze of trees on block of flats; Marylebone, London; 1903.

Stone Houses

491 Boulder-built longhouse, farmhouse and byre; Rhydymain, Gwynedd.

492 Granite cottage with sandstone dressings; Kennethmont, Aberdeenshire.

493 Farmhouse; Newstead, Yorkshire.

494 Limestone house and porch; Bibury, Gloucestershire.

495 Picturesque limestone cottage; Oakhill, Somerset.

496 Limestone chequered with brick; Stockton, Wiltshire.

497 Ashlar limestone; Oundle, Northamptonshire.

498 Millstone grit weavers' houses; Saddleworth, Yorkshire.

499 Flint with white brick; Mildenhall, Suffolk.

500 Flint banded with red brick; Bulford, Wiltshire.

501 Sandstone farmhouse; Hawnby, Yorkshire.

491					
492	493	494	498	499	500
495	496	497		501	
					502
			503		

502 Ashlar sandstone; Alyth, Perthshire.

503 Chalk (or clunch) with brick; Burnham Overy, Norfolk.

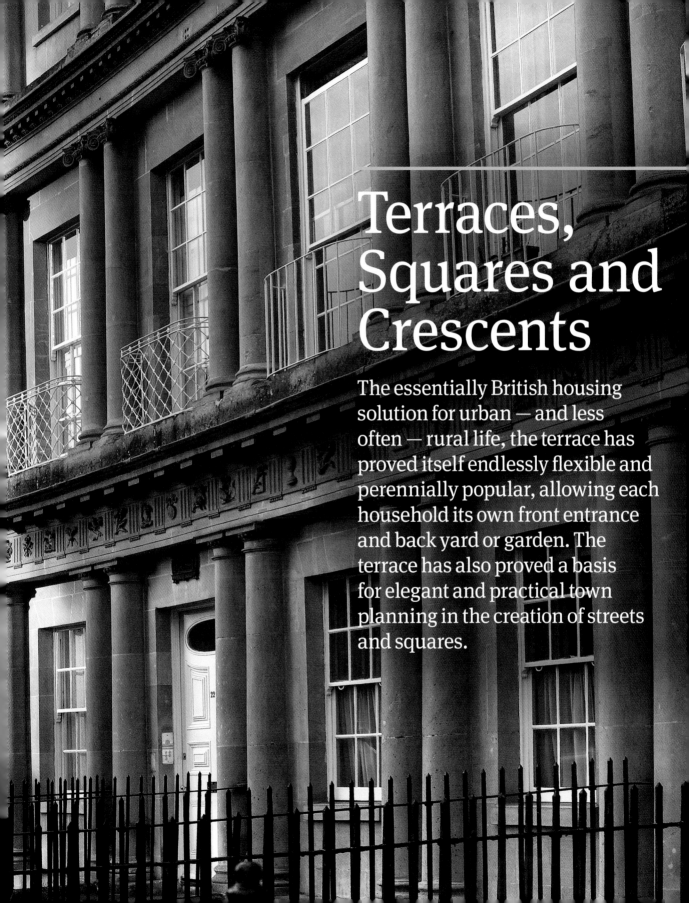

Terraces, Squares and Crescents

The essentially British housing solution for urban — and less often — rural life, the terrace has proved itself endlessly flexible and perennially popular, allowing each household its own front entrance and back yard or garden. The terrace has also proved a basis for elegant and practical town planning in the creation of streets and squares.

Terraces, Squares and Crescents

Terrace housing is a row of individual houses bonded together and unified in design to appear as a single unit, emphasising conformity over variation. Terraces are usually straight, but they were also built into squares and curved into crescents, or more rarely into a complete circle to form a 'circus'. One of the beauties of the terrace was that it could be built on hills and slopes following the lines of the landscape, thus providing views of hills and sea as at Bath, Brighton and Buxton. Terraces have ranged from the sumptuously palatial to the meanly minimal, but each house always has its own front entrance, the canvas on which much decorative energy was focused. Whether a two-up two-down, or rising to five or six storeys from basement to attic, terrace accommodation is vertical, with a few rooms at each level. In some cases the house neatly separates the family from its servants, who invariably inhabited the lowest and topmost floors, the former with their own basement entrance. Previously referred to as 'rows', the word terrace was first used by the Adam Brothers for their 1768 speculation, The Adelphi, aptly describing the garden terrace at the back of the houses that provided a promenade overlooking the Thames.

The joined row of individual houses intended for clergy of Vicar's Close, Wells built in 1348 could be considered the earliest terrace housing in Britain. However the north facade of Queen Square, Bath, built in 1728 by John Wood, is generally seen as a pioneering pattern, since the row of houses along the north side of the square is presented as the facade of an opulent Palladian mansion with a central pediment, fluted pilasters and Corinthian capitals. Terraces followed current architectural style: Queen Anne and early Georgian terraces were punctuated by projecting canopies and pedimented doorcases, but by the end of the century facades were smooth with fanlight doors set within arched openings. On Regency terraces the emphasis was on uninterrupted stucco facades, enlivened by the graphic effects of ornamental iron balconies and railings.

504 Stucco terrace of large Italianate houses, c. 1840. The stucco would originally have been stone-coloured but brightly coloured paints became from the 1960s onwards a sign of gentrification. Notting Hill Gate, West London.

505 Early 19C terrace, built c. 1810 of ashlar stone with the ground floor heavily rusticated. Edinburgh.

As the 19th century progressed the elaborate gamut of Victorian eclecticism was thrown at the terrace: Italianate rustication, balustrading and pillared portico porches; polychrome brick patterning; French Empire-style mansard roofs and iron roof cresting; dark red brick with terra-cotta panels in Gothic or Flemish Revival. By the end of the century terraces were often built to appear as a sequence of semi-detached houses, with bays, gables and porches.

At the end of the 19th century a large proportion of Britons from all classes lived in terrace houses. Constructed in multiples they were generally speculative projects whose builder carefully calculated his market and price to maximize profits while also conforming to current building regulations. Terrace housing of exceptionally high density was achieved in Victorian back-to-back terraces, built for the working class mainly in the industrial North and Midlands. The houses' usual pattern was to be split vertically, each one only looking out in one direction and eliminating ventilation. Without any back yard many tasks such as clothes-drying were done in the street or in a communal area. By the 20th century virtually all city authorities had banned back-to-back terraces, but by then these and the thousands of cheaply built terraces had already given terrace housing a bad name.

In the 1960s the large-scale demolition of thousands of Victorian terraces in cities such as Manchester led in some cases to their replacement with slab blocks of flats with doors that opened off walkways at each level, the so-called 'streets in the sky' that were intended to replicate the intimate neighbourliness of the terrace. The failure of these projects led to the realisation that the terrace is perfectly capable of reinvention in the late 20th century, and to a new appreciation of the earlier magnificent examples of terrace housing that gave British towns and cities their distinctive look.

506 The grandest of terraces, originally 31 houses, designed by John Nash: a gleaming stucco temple with giant Ionic columns, balustrading and a pediment crowded with sculpture representing Britannia crowned by Fame, built in 1826. Regents Park, London.

507 One of the many late 18C and early 19C squares to be built in a fast-growing London. It is unusual in that it is in an Elizabethan Revival style with gables and moulded windows with mullions and drip moulds. The cast-iron railings are distinctly Victorian in style. Islington, North London.

508 Victorian stone terrace of mill workers' housing built alongside the canal, in small town dominated by the wool industry, then at its peak. Marsden, Yorkshire.

509 Victorian terrace and garden wall built of the town's distinctive red bricks, the gate piers surmounted with terra-cotta ornaments that were also made locally from the adjacent clay pits. The

506	508	509
507	510 511	512

slate on the roofs and continuous porch would have come from North Wales. Ruabon, Clwyd.

510 Back-to-back terrace housing cheaply built for an industrial workforce continued in Yorkshire long after they were banned elsewhere. They accounted for about 65 per cent of

houses built in the 1880s in towns such as Bradford, Halifax and Leeds. Hyde Park, Leeds, Yorkshire.

511 A late Victorian brick terrace, the gables ornamented with decorative terra-cotta sections impressed with foliage. These, together with pantiles and the pointed ridge tiles would all

have been manufactured in the town. Bridgewater, Somerset.

512 Infill: a terrace of small houses on hillside, with local stone garden walling, slate roofs and timber cladding, built 2006. Kingsbridge, Devon.

Terra cotta

An alternative to cutting and rubbing brick to provide decorative embellishments was to make sections of ornamental terra cotta. Clay was fired in patterned moulds to produce a material which was denser and harder than brick, but of the same basic natural material which thus combined well with it.

A few grand Tudor houses, such as Sutton Place and Layer Marney, had terra-cotta detail on, for example, window frames and parapets (possibly made by Italian craftsmen), but it was never widely used during this period. In the 18th century a stone-coloured version of terra cotta was marketed by Eleanor Coade (see Coade stone).

When stucco fell from fashion in the 1860s an interest in terra cotta re-emerged, together with all types of ornamental brickwork and general polychrome effects. Terra cotta was mainly manufactured in deep red, buff (popular in the 1880s) or a greyish white. Essentially used in urban situations as its smooth surface repelled soot to some extent, terra cotta was also cheaper and lighter than ornamental stone (the blocks of terra cotta were cast hollow and then filled with concrete when in place). However, terra cotta could warp in firing and was therefore unreliable for use on large sections such as window frames and door surrounds. Among the leading producers were Doulton, Blashfield's of Stamford (who took over the remains of the Coade business) and Edwards' of Ruabon.

Characteristic terra-cotta details were plaques with Aesthetic Movement sunflowers, pots of lilies, Renaissance Revival swags and festoons or fashionable *japonaiseries*, such as oriental-style frets. It was also used for ornamental roof finials and chimney pots, particularly those moulded with Elizabethan revival or Old English patterns, such as barley-sugar twists or fleurs de lys. It was also well suited to impressive name plaques and datestones for blocks of mansion flats or workers' dwellings.

513 Terra-cotta cresting on gatehouse, ornamented with dolphins, egg-and-dart and guilloche patterns; Layer Marney, Essex; c. 1520.

514 Terra-cotta quoins and black-and-red diaper brickwork; Sutton Place, Surrey; late 16C.

513		515	516	
514		517		518
		519	520	521

515 Portrait medallion and plant-ornamented window arch on terrace; Maida Vale, London; c. 1850s–60s.

516 Balcony, window surrounds and cornice ornament in two-colour terra cotta; Mayfair, London; c. 1890s.

517 Gothic Revival leaf quatrefoil over window; Whitby, Yorkshire; c. 1860.

518 Cornice sections with gadroon pattern and key pattern on artist's studio; St John's Wood, London; late 19C.

519 Door jamb, guilloche pattern and scrolling foliage; Knightsbridge, London; 1891.

520 Cornice blocks with festoons and winged mask; Hampstead, London; c. 1890.

521 Datestone and potted sunflower; Hampstead, London; 1874.

Timber-frame

The methods of building with timber-frame reveal themselves when looking at the exteriors of houses and cottages. It was a slow development from primitive hut building to the creation of substantial dwellings. The fundamental problem was to create a walled, roofed space without filling the interior with supports (aisle posts) and beams.

One of the earliest was construction with 'cruck' beams. Single, curved pieces of wood were split in two and then erected — like wishbones — to be held fast by a ridge beam that created a roof ridge and held the structure securely. Once this was achieved the infilling of the bay (space between the upright beams) could be done from wattle and daub, made from whatever was locally available. The limitation of this system lay in its dependence on the availability of lengths of curved timber, and the difficulty in obtaining any height.

Regional differences are marked but the two basic construction types are generally known as post-and-truss and box-frame. Both involved setting the beams at right angles with the roof supported by purlins (beams running from roof ridge to eave) and tie beams (which created the base of the triangle, holding the roof rigid). King posts and crown posts linked the tie beam to the roof ridge or purlins. These methods allowed space for a proper upper floor and for the creation of jetties. While the jetty has practical uses, it can also be grand and decorative and it has always been the most imitated — and impressive — feature in the vocabulary of timber-framing.

The arrangement of beams may have been driven by their function, but the effects were also decorative and by the late 16th century, particularly in the Shropshire area, there were ostentatious displays of timber patterns that bore no relation to load-bearing requirements.

522 Cruck frame on medieval cottage; Osmaston, Derbyshire.

523 Small-panel framing on manor house; Lower Brockhampton House, Worcestershire; 14C.

524 Close-studded timber-framing with jettied gable end; Manuden, Essex.

525 Detail of pegged joints; Manuden, Essex.

526 Timber-bracing around windows, limed wood and limewashed plaster; Lavenham, Suffolk.

527 Carved beam; Paycocke's, Coggeshall, Essex; c. 1500.

528 Close-panelling with ornamental infilling; Ludlow, Shropshire; 1619.

529 Brick nogging below jetty; Colchester, Essex; 16C.

530 Jettied timber-frame houses; Lavenham, Suffolk.

531 Close-studded façade; Stoke-by-Nayland, Suffolk.

Timber-frame as Ornament

While bargeboards were a key element in giving a house or cottage a picturesque look in the early 19th century, half-timbering or timber-framing (with which bargeboards are originally associated) was assimilated until a little later. Decorative timber-frame, often used in conjunction with render, was a popular choice for estate cottages and model villages.

It was also one of the features picked out from the vernacular vocabulary by the architects of the Arts and Crafts movement, for example, Richard Norman Shaw who created gables and jetties patterned with timbers on his large country houses. Some Arts and Crafts houses, as can be expected, had genuine structural timber-frames. M. Hugh Baillie Scott built such a cottage at Findon 'because it seemed peculiarly adapted to a district where its cost was no greater than a nine-inch brick wall'.

The Edwardians showed a great sentimentality towards the countryside: publishers, illustrators and postcard manufacturers produced numerous images of traditional country cottages, a large proportion of which were half-timbered. Some derelict old cottages were pillaged for beams that were incorporated into new houses, and the fashion for emphasising beams with black paint dates from this period. For the speculative builder in the suburbs, a slice of romantic country life could be suggested with the application of beam patterns on the exterior, even if it was on a block of flats with nine floors. Thus the much-derided Mock-Tudor style was born.

By the end of the 20th century houses were still being decorated with applied wood 'half-timbered' gables, presumably because this detail had become deeply embedded in the nation's psyche as a symbol of home.

532 Timber-frame ornament on turrets and gables, cream paint and pebbledash; Waddesdon, Buckinghamshire; c. 1880s.

533 Mock Tudor flats; Highgate, London; c. 1928–30.

534 Black-and-white timber-frame decoration at roof level; Grim's Dyke, Harrow, London; 1872.

		534	535	
532		536		537
533			538	539
			540	541

535 Double cottage with timber-frame, tile-hanging, stone and brick; Ticehurst, Kent; mid-19C.

536 Double cottage painted with timber-framing patterns; Bridgenorth, Shropshire; late 19C.

537 Cottage with wavy-edge beams; Kingswood, Surrey; early 20C.

538 End-of-terrace house in half timber with jetty and fake pegged joints; Port Sunlight, Cheshire; c. 1900.

539 Suburban house with matching garage, diamond-leaded casement windows; Epsom, Surrey; 1930s.

540 Block of flats; Maida Vale, London; 1930s.

541 Diamond-pane windows and timber-framing on housing development; Maldon, Essex; 2000.

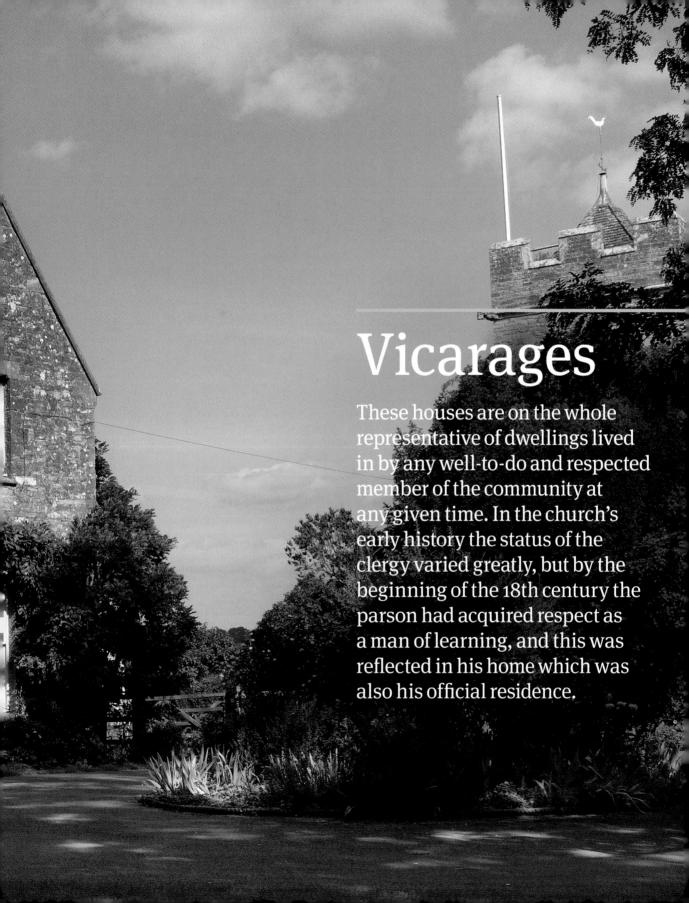

Vicarages

These houses are on the whole
representative of dwellings lived
in by any well-to-do and respected
member of the community at
any given time. In the church's
early history the status of the
clergy varied greatly, but by the
beginning of the 18th century the
parson had acquired respect as
a man of learning, and this was
reflected in his home which was
also his official residence.

Vicarages

The parochial system, whereby lords of the manor built churches and appointed priests as incumbents of the parish, evolved over hundreds of years from the 7th century onwards. The general term for the spiritual overseer was a parson, but he could be a rector or a vicar. The difference between a rector and a vicar depends on the history of his benefice or living. In simple terms a rector had a right to collect tithes from the parish — the corn, grain, hay etc. was his 'living'. During the 11th century many churches were donated, as acts of piety, to the monasteries that enjoyed the benefits of the tithes and installed clerks to perform services. By the 13th century popes and bishops, anxious at this development, instituted vicars as religious deputies. Thus the vicar was below the rector in the religious pecking order. From Norman times church hierarchy dictated that the bishop live in an appropriately imposing palace beside his cathedral. Around the cathedral close, in fine houses, lived the dean and canons, members of the cathedral chapter. The late 14th-century vicar's closes, as at Wells and Chichester, were lodgings for vicars choral, who were required to take the place at services of absentee canons and prebends. It was recognised that ideally a parish should have a house for the priest — a parsonage, rectory or vicarage — and glebe land (land assigned to the incumbent as part of his benefice). After the Dissolution Henry VIII granted or sold the majority of the livings that had belonged to the monasteries but, whoever had patronage of the living, it was the duty of the incumbent to be responsible for its maintenance.

    After the Reformation it was possible for priests in the Church of England to marry. Slowly the living standards of the clergy improved, some helped perhaps by a wife and family to housekeep and farm the glebe land. As parsons became better educated the status of the parsonage gradually equalled that of a small manor or prosperous yeoman's farmhouse.

542 Rear elevation of the vicarage which leads through a Gothic gateway arch into the churchyard. Built of local stone, granite and Cornish Delabole slate in the 1850s. Feock, Cornwall.

543 One of a terrace of houses built in the mid 14C for the vicars acting as vice-prebendaries attached to Wells Cathedral. The walled front gardens were established in the early 15C and entered through a battlemented doorway leading off the street. The chimney is carved with two shields of arms. Wells, Somerset.

The Queen Anne's Bounty fund established in 1704 (raised from tithes grabbed by Henry VIII) was set up to help poorer clergymen to live in appropriate accommodation. But during the secular atmosphere of the Georgian period church property of all types fell into disrepair, a state that the 1776 Clergy Residences Repair Act tried to redress. This enabled the clergy to raise money for repair or even a new house by mortgaging the income from their benefices. The resulting elegant and substantial Georgian parsonages were ideal for younger sons of the aristocracy and gentry, for whom a career in the church was the only alternative to the army or navy.

In contrast to the Georgians the 19th-century churchmen were keen to endow their parsonages with appropriate features in an appropriate style. Characteristic were P. F. Robinson's plans for parsonages in *Village Architecture* (1830) that suggested they should be 'in the Old English character' and although a little ornament might be employed it should be 'modest and unassuming...the open porch

544 Known as the Treasurer's House because the Treasurer of Wells Cathedral was made rector and lived here in 1226. The two light mullion windows with cusped cinquefoil heads light the hall and date from c. 1330. Martock, Somerset.

545 Vicarage built between the 15C and 18C. In view is the 15C timber-framed range ending with the 16C brick stepped gable. Methwold, Norfolk.

546 A parsonage house beside the church, its exterior revealing the work of several periods, but the effect being principally Georgian with a classical frontage under a small pediment. Dormington, Herefordshire.

547 The front elevation of a substantial three-storey rectory added in the early 19C to an earlier house. The rector had only the care of a small Saxon church in a remote village. Duntisborne Rouse, Gloucestershire.

548 Impressive Gothic Revival vicarage, built in 1861 alongside the new church (now demolished) both designed by John Johnson. Fashionable polychrome effects achieved by mixing yellow stock brick with stone, a deeper yellow and red bricks. Camden Town, London.

549 Plain Georgian parsonage built of millstone grit in 1779 with a pedimented doorcase and sash windows. Here the Brontë sisters lived with their clergyman father. Haworth, Yorkshire.

550 Red-brick rectory, c.1809, a living in the gift of the Earl of Leicester of Holkham Hall and one of several rectories built by the estate in the same style. Burnham Market, Norfolk.

551 Victorian Gothic Revival vicarage with elaborately glazed windows echoed by the effect of the polychrome brickwork. Nantwich, Cheshire.

indicating a welcome to the poor as well as the rich'. In some cases the incumbent bought the land from the church, and the Parsonages Act of 1838 permitted him to sell it too, which explains why there might be an Old Parsonage in a town or village as well as a rectory or vicarage. The Pluralities Act of the same year tightened up the rules, and clergy were forbidden to undertake additional money-making activities such as farming or school-mastering and were required to live in their parish full-time, rather combine several livings. As a result more vicarages were built or purchased. The mid 19th-century expansion of industrial towns and cities required the church to extend its ministry rapidly. Gothic Revival style (the style of Christianity) was *de rigueur* for these new churches and accompanying vicarages, whose generous size reflected their use in spiritual, pastoral and procedural duties. In the 20th century, however, size signalled expensive maintenance and a lack of humility for the Church of England. Thousands of vicarages and rectories were sold off to become The Old Rectory or The Old Vicarage.

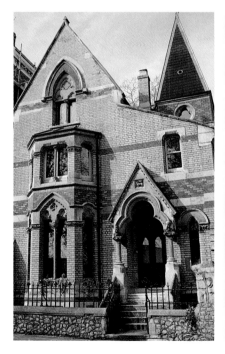

Windows

Most early window openings, such as they were, had wooden shutters on the inside, and transluccncc was achieved using materials such as linen cloth, horn or reed lattices. All precious early glass, imported from France, Flanders and parts of Germany, was used in ecclesiastical building; glazed medieval domestic windows, available only to the wealthy, were a pale imitation in shape and technique. Henry III, whose glass windows at Windsor and Woodstock are documented, issued a writ that his glass casements should be divided in two so that they could be opened 'at pleasure'. Such was the value of glass that casements were not considered a permanent fixture of a house until 1599.

By the 1570s glass was being made in Britain, notably in Surrey and Sussex where there was silica and wood for furnaces. Along with other manufacturing processes the national shortage of wood led to a ban in 1615 on its use in glass-making, whereupon it was moved to the coal-producing areas of Newcastle and the West Midlands. By the late 16th century glass was affordable for many although it remained unattainable for the poor over the next two centuries. House-owners and makers were delighted as builders created a profusion of window shapes — mullion, oriel, bay and bow — that reflected the light and made a façade sparkle.

Early windows were constructed by cutting glass into diamonds and rectangles which were supported by lead bars (known as cames). Tudor leaded lights were principally composed of diamond shapes, with occasional Gothic shapes and stained-glass sections also set within the iron frames that were hung on pivot hinges as casement windows with stone or wooden mullions. By the mid 17th century leaded glazing was generally in squares, and the windows were horizontally divided by mullions and headed with a drip mould.

The arrival of Classicism meant that windows were required to be both symmetrical and vertical, reflecting the trend for

higher ceilings. Fashion and practicality were combined: brick was increasingly the dominant building material which made the creation of vertical openings far simpler, so the new cross-head, or mullion-and-transom window emerged wherein a cross-piece cut across the mullion at the uppermost third of its height.

The invention of the sash window around 1670 was one of the most radical changes to be made to the exterior of the British house, sometimes even replacing old windows on existing houses. It was the perfect match for the symmetry of Classical architecture, as window voids could be filled evenly with modular square and rectangular panes. During the first half of the 18th century Classical motifs were applied to window surrounds: grotesque or prominent keystones, bold rustication, baroque-style volutes at the base and lugs at the top, or Palladian triangular or segmental pediments projecting over the window. Venetian and Diocletian windows were also introduced during this period.

Building regulations affected windows in several ways. Fire protection measures in the London Building Act of 1709 required that the wooden frame of a sash window be recessed by four inches rather than sit flush with the outside of the wall. This had the effect of making the window frames appear less dominant. A similar Act in 1774 then demanded that the frame be recessed into the wall, which further reduced its visibility. A window tax had been levied in 1695, which probably resulted in the creation of bi-partite windows (since two windows as close as 12 inches counted as one), and some 'blind' windows. However many of these bricked-in window spaces might equally have been there for reasons of symmetry or interior alteration. The tax was extended from 1798 to 1825 during which time it affected houses with only six windows. Builders reacted by enlarging them: some sash windows now reached almost to floor level, and the proportion of window to façade was greatly increased.

Regency architecture encouraged an easy flow between house and garden. Apart from floor-length sash windows French windows were also introduced, described by Humphry Repton in 1816 as a modern improvement 'borrowed from the French of folding glass doors opening into a garden; by which effect a room is like a tent or marquee, and in summer, delightful'. Bow windows, verandas and balconies further enhanced the light and airy feel. Fancy glazing was also in vogue: arched windows had 'gothick' arcading, loops

552 Stone-mullioned windows with leaded lights; Levens Hall, Kendal, Cumbria; late 16C/early 17C.

553 Upper storey with blind and real sash windows; Woburn, Bedfordshire; mid-18C.

554 Long casement windows with coloured glass margin on stucco terrace; Brighton, Sussex; c.1835.

555 Cemetery gate lodge with bay and central stilt-headed window; Bridlington, Yorkshire; 1879.

556 Bay window with leaded casements; Palmers Green, London; 1920s.

557 Turret window with sash fitting and leaded glazing on upper section; Hampstead, London; c.1890.

558 Steel corner window on semi-detached house; Tufnell Park, London; 1930s.

or circles. Margins of coloured glass were popular at the edges of windows and on glazed doors. On picturesque cottages, lodges or almshouses windows with glazing patterns of diamonds, hexagons, lattices and lozenges were an essential element of the style.

By the middle of the 19th century the fall in the price of glass, resulting from improved manufacturing processes, made it robust and economical enough to use in large panes on both sash windows and new large-pane casements. Smooth flat façades fell out of favour to be replaced by the interrupted line of the canted bay window which became a field for ornamentation. Small nods were made to Gothic Revival on thousands of terrace houses whose bay-window mullions were converted into colonettes capped by Gothic-inspired flowers and foliage. By contrast with the plain glass of the Victorian window itself, the surround was decorated with all manner of carved stone dressings, chamfering, moulding and polychrome brick.

The architects and the builders of the 1870s onwards ran the gamut of every window style: the 'stilt head' window became a popular new feature, but equally dormers, oriels, casement as well as sash windows were all used in a multiplicity of revival styles. For example the Queen Anne Revival style demanded a reversion to early 18th-century-style sash windows with segmental (shallow-arched) heads and to sash windows filled with many small panes. The range of window designs reflected the variety of rooms within: halls, cloakrooms, studies, studios, dining rooms, sitting rooms, etc. Windows no longer clearly indicated each storey of a house, since much was made of stairwell windows and double-height halls. Towards the end of the 19th century window design tended to divide horizontally into one-third/two-thirds, with the top third glazed in a more decorative manner and opening independently.

In stark contrast to this rich assembly of window types destined for the house, mansion block, or terrace built for the middle and upper classes, the slum-dweller's cellar window admitted virtually no natural light. Housing reformers soon realised that sunlight and ventilation were crucial to health and Victorian model housing is notable for its plain, unadorned but large windows.

House builders who were following the Arts and Crafts route at the turn of the 20th century returned to the horizontal casement window of vernacular tradition. Since the casement had connotations of cottages and rural charm, leaded lights were frequently revived, particularly when the design included any half-timbered decoration. A commentator in 1924 wrote: 'Lead lights are, of course, still very popular on account of their picturesque and old-world appearance — few suburban residents have quite forgotten the baronial hall — but in an almost endless repetition of cheap-jack medievalism they defeat their own object, and thus are characteristic only of the present day'. French windows leading into the garden became extremely popular as the garden increasingly became an extension of the house — somewhere to sit, eat and live. For the neo-Georgian style popularized by Edwin Lutyens, plain sash windows with exterior shutters were revived.

In direct contrast to the homespun Arts and Crafts look, where windows huddled to the centre of the house, in the late 1920s windows moved towards the corners and indeed around them. The 'moderne' suntrap window let as much light as possible into what was, in other respects, a traditional, suburban, semi-detached house. The picture window — a stretch of uninterrupted glass — was the 1950s solution to getting maximum light into the principal rooms: this was the British answer to the radical glass architecture of Europe and America by Modern Movement architects such as Mies van der Rohe and Marcel Breuer. Using walls of glass as a way of generating heat has also become one of the methods of building an energy-efficient house, an important issue in the late 20th and early 21st centuries.

| 555 | 557 |
| 556 | 558 |

Bay and Bow Windows

Both originally medieval forms, bay and bow windows first appeared in the 14th century, but become more frequent during the 15th. A bay window was usually built in relation to the gable. The most significant or prestigious window, a bay or bow, generally related to the great hall and held any valuable stained glass. Ostentatious use of glass was fashionable in the 16th and 17th centuries, so bay windows, and semi-circular bow windows, presented glittering façades. In London the use of bay windows was restricted during the 17th and 18th century because the wood was considered a fire hazard.

Classical Palladian-influenced façades were principally flat apart from the portico, but by the Adam period, many rear elevations were bowed, a feature which subsequently moved round to the front, and became a particular characteristic of Regency style. Carpenters and glaziers became increasingly skilled at glazing and creating sash windows for bows and bays, which also were in demand for new shop fronts. During the Regency period an enthusiasm for sunlight, air and sea views, in resorts such as Brighton and Ramsgate, made such windows very popular.

The canted bay window became almost ubiquitous on terrace housing around 1860, giving each house a more individual feel and expanding the size of the front room. At the turn of the century it was more typical for the bay to be square, and Hermann Muthesius wrote that owing to the inclemency of the British weather bay windows were 'the substitute for seating in the open air...for centuries English architects have shown a special fondness for them'. By the 1920s the suburban bay was given a distinctly modern Art Deco look by curving the walls and extending the windows horizontally. In 20th-century suburban architecture the inclusion of a bay or bow was an important distinction for private house-owners as council or charity-built properties rarely had that extra, expensive dimension.

559 Bay with stone mullion casement windows on manor house: Lytes Cary, Somerset; 1533.

560 Brick bow with stone mullion windows; Burton Agnes Hall, Yorkshire; early 17C.

559	561 562 563 564
560	565 566 567 568

561 Bay with sash windows decorated in Gothick style; Richmond, Yorkshire; late 18C.

562 Weatherboarded bay with sash windows; Hampstead, London; mid to late 18C.

563 Brick bay with casement windows; Ditcheat, Somerset; late 18C.

564 Bow with sash windows on first floor above shop premises; Winchester, Hampshire; c. 1800.

565 Bow with sash windows on stucco terrace; Brighton, Sussex; c. 1810.

566 Bay with sash windows on stucco terrace; Cheltenham, Gloucestershire; c. 1840–50.

567 Bay with cast-iron casement windows on picturesque cottage; Snitterfield, Warwickshire, c. 1840–50.

568 Thatched bay window added to stone cottage; Stoke Gabriel, Devon; 19C.

569 Bay with Wardian case (1875) on stucco terrace, Kensington, London; 1871.

570 Bay with sash windows on brick terrace with decorated stone frame; Kensington, London; c. 1870.

571 Bay with sash windows on stone terrace with moulded ornament; Bristol; c. 1880s.

572 Bay with sash windows and original external awning fitments on stone terrace; Bath; c. 1880s.

573 Bay with sash window, stone banded in brick; Cardiff; 1903.

574 Bay with sash window on stone terrace; Bath; early 20C.

575 Bay with sash windows on brick terrace; Hackney, London; c. 1890s.

576 Bay with wooden-frame sash window with decorative leaded lights; Walton-on-the-Naze, Essex; early 20C.

577 Bow, wooden-frame casement and transom windows; Evercreech, Somerset; 1930s.

578 Bay with steel-frame suntrap casement windows; Glastonbury, Somerset; 1930s.

579 Stone-frame bow with sash window, top section leaded; Cardiff; 1920s.

580 Stone-mullioned window with wooden casements; Hopton, Derbyshire.

581 Timber-mullioned window with leaded casements on timber-frame house; Lavenham, Suffolk; medieval.

582 Wooden-frame cross-head window with casements; Abinger Hammer, Surrey; c. 1660.

583 Metal casement window, set in concrete frame; Chelmsford, Essex; 1950s.

584 Stone-mullioned window with drip mould over leaded casements; Martock, Somerset; 17C.

585 Wooden casement set in brick and stone; Knightsbridge, London; c. 1880.

586 Wooden-frame casement windows, including dormer and bow; Gidea Park, Essex; 1912.

587 Steel casement windows; Twickenham, London; 1930s.

Casements and Mullions

The casement was the earliest form of fixed window and it remained the norm for cottages and vernacular buildings. The term casement literally refers to the framed section that holds the glass in place, so can also apply to a bow, bay, dormer or oriel. A casement window was hinged at the side and in Britain it generally opened outwards although where there are working shutters it may open inwards. The verticals supporting the casements, which may be stone or wood, are termed mullions. Moulded stone mullions often appear in conjunction with a drip-mould over the top designed to protect the casement from the wet. Casements are unsuitable for large areas of glass and are difficult to use where verticality is the desired effect, hence the popularity of the sash window.

For an upright (rather than a landscape) window a transom (horizontal bar) was added. This may be called a cross-head window. Typically, 20th-century housing had a transom window: the upper section usually opened out from the top and was often separately decorated with coloured glass. To bring maximum light into a house with casement windows several would often be placed in a row: this was a common feature of Arts and Crafts houses and flats. The design of modern steel-framed windows was based on the basic casement type. The steel-framed window, an essential feature in the glass-and-steel building of the Modern Movement, was the next revolution, introduced around 1920. Its advantages were clear: unlike wood it could fit tightly, it could be ordered in manufactured standard units complete with fittings and pivoting hinges were developed which meant that the whole window could be cleaned from the inside (a particularly important consideration for flat-dwellers). Steel windows did rust, but it was discovered that this could be prevented in the late 1930s by galvanising the entire frame with zinc. The most prominent feature was the horizontally glazed, 'streamlined' metal window (for which Crittall was the principal supplier). Post-war, the mass-produced metal window was as functional and as economical as possible, often reduced to a simple opening casement or side-sliding sash windows in limited sizes.

	583
580 581 582	584 585 586 587

Sash Windows

Primitive sash windows already existed in France, but the sash window that opened smoothly with a system of pulleys and counterweights and that effectively eliminated both draughts and awkward inward or outward openings, was probably a British invention of around 1670, discussed with enthusiasm even at the august level of the Royal Society. Early examples often had segmental or swept-head tops; the glazing bars were relatively thick (two inches) and the panes of glass small, as many as four or five across. Over the next century these were reduced in width and elegantly moulded. There are plenty of exceptions but as a general rule mid-Georgian sash windows had six-over-six, or eight-over-eight panes. Regency and early 19th-century sash windows were usually four-over-four, sometimes with a margin or border or with decorative curved and arched glazing bars. Improved glass manufacture reduced panes to two-over-two, and finally just one large pane over another (a strengthening 'horn' or bracket at the base of each upper frame compensated for the extra weight). Patterned glazing and coloured glass was revived for the top section only on late Victorian and Edwardian sash windows.

Side-sliding sash windows (an unsophisticated version of the form) usually appeared on cottages or village houses. Unlike a proper sash window these did not need the complicated weight-and-pulley mechanism. This pattern was very common in late 20th-century aluminium-frame windows.

588 Side-sliding sash window; Market Overton, Rutland; 19C.

589 Coloured glass top section sash window on brick terrace; Holloway, London; 1898.

590 9-on-6-pane unrecessed sash window with internal shutters; Bristol; 1709–11.

591 6-on-6-pane unrecessed sash window with segmental head on terrace; Chelsea, London; mid-18C.

592 2-on-2-pane with margin lights on stucco terrace; Regent's Park, London; c. 1820.

593 Arched sash with margin lights on stucco terrace; Notting Hill, London; c. 1835.

594 4-on-4 pane sash window with separate side lights, stone terrace; Clifton, Bristol; 1820–30.

595 3-on-3-pane sash window on stone cottage; Grasmere, Cumbria; 19C.

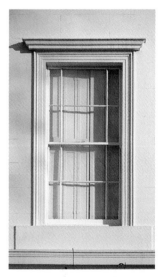

Classical Windows

The Venetian window is tripartite with a central arched window flanked by two straight-headed smaller sidelights. Venetian windows are also called Palladian, even though Palladio was only one among many who used them.

Employed by Donato Bramante and other Italian Renaissance architects the Venetian window was introduced in England in the 17th century. Prior to the general adoption of the sash window the shape also appeared traced on leaded casement windows. By the 1720s the Venetian window was one of the hallmarks of grand Palladian architecture, but it also became one of the most popular motifs of the 18th century, appearing on thousands of ordinary Georgian houses. Isaac Ware described them in 1756 in his *Complete Body of Architecture* as 'calculated for shew, and very pompous in their nature; and when executed with judgement, of extreme elegance'. As the entire triple opening counted as one window the Venetian represented good value for purposes of window taxation. It subsequently appeared in the late 19th and early 20th centuries as one of a range of interesting window shapes, for example as a small hall window beside the front door.

The Diocletian window is named for the ancient Baths of Diocletian in Rome from which the Italian Renaissance architects took their inspiration. Lunette-shaped with two vertical glazing bars, it was nearly always used on top or attic storeys or at basement level.

Circular windows (also called medallion, bull's eye or *œil de bœuf*) appear at the same time, although their shape necessarily limited their use. They were also rather more baroque than suited the general taste, but were perfect for pediments and for use in conjunction with elaborate features such as domes and cupolas. As a quirky shape they appeared erratically at all periods particularly in halls and stairwells.

596 Venetian shape in leaded casement windows; Hadleigh, Suffolk; 1676.

597 Diocletian window above Venetian window; Saltram, Plymouth, Devon; 18C.

596		598	599	
597		600	601	602
		603	604	605

598 Double Venetian window; Rokeby Hall, Yorkshire; c.1730.

599 Venetian window on gate lodge; Prior Park, Bath; 18C.

600 Venetian windows on town house; Broad Street, Ludlow, Shropshire; c. 1760.

601 Venetian ground-floor hall window on semi-detached; Acton, London; c. 1912.

602 Diocletian windows on estate cottages; Harewood, Yorkshire; late 18C.

603 Neo-Georgian Diocletian window; Hampshire; 1989.

604 Circular window on lodge; Charborough, Dorset; 1790.

605 Neo-Georgian circular window; Holland Park, London; 1950s–1960s.

Dormer and Oriel Windows

Dormers originally appeared on steep Gothic roofs, but were equally typical on the high roofs of the Classical late 17th century, Queen Anne or early Georgian houses. If a house had a mansard roof, it almost inevitably had dormer windows. Often windows of convenience rather than design, dormers were frequently inserted later, for example in cottages to provide extra height at upper-floor level. They were an economical way of creating an upper floor in a single-storey building and were particularly characteristic of long, low Scottish cottages and bungalows with one upper room. Half-dormers occurred when the window base was in the wall, but the top protruded from the roof. The deep roofs of the Arts and Crafts style frequently incorporated dormer windows.

Most dormers emerged from the roof on a small gable, but there are examples dating from the early 20th century where the roof was curved to create an 'eyebrow' over the top of the window, an effect common in thatch and imitated with tile. A roof-light, by contrast, had the window let into the pitch of the roof.

Oriels (projecting upper-level windows) appeared on both stone and timber-framed medieval houses. Being a prominent feature the oriel window was often decorated with heraldic devices or Gothic ornamentation, and was roofed or surmounted with a castellated or pierced frieze. Usually three-sided, it could also be five-sided. It was often placed in line with the dais in the great hall. Its usefulness as a look-out made the oriel a favourite on gatehouses and lodges. Oriel windows were often made to take advantage of a particular view of sea or landscape.

Eighteenth- and 19th-century oriel windows usually had Gothic or Gothic Revival ornamentation in reference to the origin of the form, and were often later additions to the main structure. At the end of the 19th century the oriel was a favourite window in Queen Anne style, stripped of all Gothic associations. Twentieth-century suburban terrace and semi-detached houses also sometimes featured small triangular oriels that conferred added glamour.

606 Oriel window on manor house; Great Chalfield, Wiltshire; late 15C.

607 Dormer window on barns converted to cottages; Arlington Row, Bibury, Gloucestershire; 14C building, 16C/17C dormers.

| 606 | 608 609 610 611 |
| 607 | 612 613 614 615 |

608 Dormer windows on town house; Salisbury, Wiltshire; late 17C.

609 Gothick-style oriel on brick terrace; Hampstead, London; later addition to house (c.1800).

610 Dormer on whitewashed stone cottage; Kirkmichael, Ayrshire; 19C.

611 Half-dormer on stone cottage; Newton-by-the-Sea, Northumberland; 19C.

612 Gothick-style oriel; Cheltenham, Gloucestershire; c.1820–30.

613 Double-height Arts and Crafts oriels on studio house; Chelsea, London; 1893–94.

614 Arts and Crafts oriel with decorative plasterwork; Hampstead, London; 1895.

615 Dormers on terrace; Port Sunlight, Cheshire; 1890s.

Unusual Windows

616 Gable window; Hampstead, London; c.1885.

617 Sash window on brick terrace; Cambridge; c. 1840.

618 Steel window with concrete rustic lintel; Smithfield, London; 1980s.

619 Wooden-frame window on circular house; A La Ronde, Exmouth, Devon; 1798.

620 Carved stone basement window; Burford, Oxfordshire; c. 1700.

Experimentation with quirkily shaped windows was usually confined to lighting odd spots in houses such as halls, stairwells, attics, or to unconventional polygonal buildings.

Interest in exotic styles, a theme of the late 18th and early 19th centuries, also contributed to the genre, and windows with scalloped or ogee-arched heads appeared styled as 'Hindoo', 'Oriental' or 'Chinese'. Although these were more common in incidental garden buildings they are most likely to appear in frivolous small lodges and gatehouses. The exploration of new ways of building, for example in siting houses underground, present a challenge to find new solutions in window shapes.

621 Staircase window; Cirencester, Gloucestershire; early 20C.

622 Semi-circular window bisected by division between two terrace houses; East Finchley, London; 1930s.

623 Non-opening window with ventilation louvre at base; Haddenham, Buckinghamshire; 1960s.

624 Window lighting underground house; Tetbury, Gloucestershire; 1990s.

			619	620	621
616	617	618	622 623		624

index of names and places

index of illustrations

Front cover and pp.112–13: Medieval stone manor house, with later additions. The limewashed central bay was built c. 1540, the wing to the left is dated 1616 with bay windows topped with castellations. Owlpen Manor, Gloucestershire. (Photo Philippa Lewis)

Back cover, clockwise from top left: see illustrations 407, 461, 88, 164

pp. 2–3: Stone Georgian country house, built in the Palladian style in 1770, to designs by the architect Sir Robert Taylor. Set in parkland thought to have been planned by Capability Brown. The façade with its canted bay looks over the River Dart. Sharpham House, Devon. (Photo Kim Sayer)

pp. 22–23: Post-war public housing, two from the sequence of five slab blocks of flats standing in parkland, built by the London County Council in 1958–59, and designed by the Architecture Department. Modernist in style and standing on piloti the plan is influenced by Le Corbusier. Alton Estate West, Roehampton, South-west London. (Photo Gillian Darley)

pp. 42–43: 1920s bungalow in suburban setting showing original bay window with leaded casement windows and clinker garden wall. Typically it has been extended c. 1975, with an extra room to one side beside the front door, and with an integral garage to the other. The original garage would have been detached and on a smaller scale. Ewell, Surrey. (Photo Philippa Lewis)

pp. 58–59: A grain warehouse constructed in 1866–68, to designs by G.F. Lyster, this was originally one of three enclosing the dock basin; converted into flats from 1989 onwards. Waterloo Dock, Liverpool. (Photo Kim Sayer)

pp. 66–67: A thatched stone cottage, probably 18C with additions from both gable ends built to meet 20C living requirements. Milton, Wiltshire. (Photo Philippa Lewis)

pp. 92–93: 19C farmhouse and a cluster of stone-built barns and byres in a sheltered valley position, the lowland pasture enclosed with dry stone walls. St John's in the Vale, Cumbria. (Photo Kim Sayer)

pp. 126–27: Victorian gate lodge that guards the entrance gates, both pedestrian and vehicular, from the village high street into the park of Badminton House. Built c. 1860 in a Tudor Gothic style the lodge has casement windows with diamond panes, gabled oriel window and finial gables. Great Badminton, Gloucestershire. (Photo Philippa Lewis)

pp. 142–43: Semi-detached house c. 1910 with a façade of tile-hanging, pebbledash and brick and double-height bays with leaded casement windows. Built in an area that rapidly developed after local landowners sold large tracts of land for development in 1902. Palmer's Green, North London. (Photo Emily Cole)

pp. 154–55: Architect John Wood the Elder designed The Circus of terrace houses. It is entered by three separate streets, so the facing view is always an uninterrupted curve. Built in 1754 each storey is marked by a different order, from Roman Doric, Ionic up to Corinthian. Bath, Somerset. (Photo Philippa Lewis)

pp. 166–67: A typical plain stone Victorian vicarage, built in 1867, one of at least 200 built to designs by architect Ewan Christian. Compton Dundon, Somerset. (Photo Philippa Lewis)

Photo Credits
All photographs are from the Edifice Photo Library (www.edificephoto.com) and are taken by Gillian Darley and Philippa Lewis except for the following:

Emily Cole 101,136, 282, 342, 466, 556
Liz Dunnell 180, 187
Adrienne Hart-Davis 452
Sarah Jackson 79
Andy Keate 153, 498, 508
Charlotte Mellis 137
Sally-Ann Norman 57, 597
Clare Pawley 147
Tom Thistlethwaite 96, 306
Eddie Ryle-Hodges 118, 139, 142, 254, 365, 417, 598, 615
Kim Sayer 11, 395, 461, 603
Larraine Worpole 26, 624

A Note on Captions
The photographs in this book can be identified by number (1–624). Please refer to the maps at top right on each double page to locate the pictures. We have tried to date the houses and their details as accurately as possible, however this was not always feasible from the evidence to hand. We shall be pleased to make any additions or corrections in future editions.

Prestel Verlag, Munich. A member of Verlagsgruppe Random House GmbH

Prestel Verlag
Neumarkter Str. 28, 81673 Munich
Tel. +49 (0)89-4136-0
Fax +49 (0)89-4136-2335
www.prestel.de

Prestel Publishing Ltd.
4, Bloomsbury Place, London WC1A 2QA
Tel. +44 (020) 7323 5004
Fax +44 (020) 7636 8004

Prestel Publishing
900 Broadway, Suite 603, New York, NY 10003
Tel. +1 (212) 995-2720
Fax +1 (212) 995-2733
www.prestel.com

Library of Congress Control Number: 2010941109; British Library Cataloguing-in-Publication Data: a catalogue record for this book is available from the British Library; Deutsche Nationalbibliothek holds a record of this publication in the Deutsche Nationalbibliografie; detailed bibliographical data can be found under: http://dnb.d-nb.de

Prestel books are available worldwide. Please contact your nearest bookseller or one of the above addresses for information concerning your local distributor.

Editorial direction: Philippa Hurd
Design, layout and typesetting: sugarfree, London, 020 7619 7430
Production: Friederike Schirge
Origination: Repro Ludwig, Zell am See
Printing and binding: C&C Printing

MIX
Paper from responsible sources
FSC® C008047

Verlagsgruppe Random House FSC-DEU-0100
The FSC®-certified paper Chinese Golden Sun matt art is produced by mill Sun Paper Group (Yanzhou Tianzhang Paper Industry Co. Ltd.) in Shandong, PRC.

Printed in China

ISBN 978-3-7913-4556-7